Delighting in the Sunlit Uplands of Grace

Spurgeon on Joy

C. H. SPURGEON
COMPILED BY MALCOLM MACLEAN

CHRISTIAN
HERITAGE

Scripture quotations are taken from the *King James Version.*

Some Scripture quotations taken directly from Spurgeon's writings reflect the *King James Version* but are worded slightly differently. They have been left as Spurgeon wrote them.

Introduction Copyright © Christian George 2015
Copyright © Christian Focus Publications 2015

paperback ISBN 978-1-78191-586-8
epub ISBN 978-1-78191-700-8
mobi ISBN 978-1-78191-701-5

Published in 2015
in the
Christian Heritage Imprint
of
Christian Focus Publications Ltd,
Geanies House, Fearn, Ross-shire,
IV20 1TW, Scotland, UK.
www.christianfocus.com

Cover design by Daniel van Straaten

Printed by Bell and Bain, Glasgow

CONTENTS

CONTENTS

Introduction

By Christian George

On the evening of New Year's Eve, 1891, Charles Spurgeon delivered a brief speech to a small group of friends in Mentone, France. "We have come so far on the journey of life," he said, "and, standing at the boundary of another year, we look back."

For the 57-year-old London pastor, there was much to look back upon. In less than four decades, Spurgeon had preached in person to an estimated ten million people. He had published more words in the English language than any Christian author in history. Fifty-six million copies of his sermons were in circulation, many having been translated into more than 40 languages.

His magnum opus – a commentary on the Psalms that took 20 years to complete – had been widely applauded. The Metropolitan Tabernacle saw a weekly attendance of 6,000 members, and 14,654 people had been baptized over the years. Sixty-six ministries had spawned under Spurgeon's guidance: a theological college, two orphanages, a book fund, a retirement home, a clothing drive, a Sunday school for the blind, a ministry to policemen, and dozens more.

Few pastors in the history of Protestant Christianity could lay claim to the sheer number of ministerial endeavors and successes as could the "Prince of Preachers," Charles Haddon Spurgeon.

And yet, only four weeks before his death, Spurgeon's words were flavored with confession. "I look back, and remember what I might have done and have not done; what opportunities of usefulness I have not seized; what sins I have allowed to pass unrebuked; what struggling beginners in grace I have failed to help." For Spurgeon, humility was not occasional; it was continual – and essential!

From the beginnings of his ministry as a young "Essex bumpkin" to its crescendo in the New Park Street Chapel and its grand finale in the Down Grade Controversy, the "Lion of London" that God had brought into this world only ten days after the great Baptist missionary William Carey died, tempered his achievements with a profound sense of joyful unworthiness.

But at the age of 22, Charles Spurgeon almost quit the ministry. He and Susannah had been married less than one year. Their sons, Charles and Thomas, were infants. After three years in the big city, Spurgeon's ministry had solicited envy from his opponents, admiration from the evangelicals, and criticism from the press. Susannah often hid the morning newspaper to prevent Charles from reading its headlines.

On the evening of October 19, 1856, Spurgeon's popularity had forced the rental of the Surrey Garden Music Hall in order to hold the 12,000 people congregated inside. Ten thousand eager listeners stood outside the building, scrambling to hear his sermon. The event constituted one of the largest crowds gathered to hear a nonconformist preacher – a throwback to the days of George Whitefield.

A few minutes after 6 o'clock, someone in the audience shouted, "Fire! The galleries are giving way! The place is falling!" Pandemonium ensued as a balcony collapsed. Those trying to get into the building blocked the exit of those fighting to escape. Spurgeon attempted to quell the commotion, but to no avail. His text for the day was Proverbs 3:33, "The curse of the Lord is in the house of the wicked" – a verse he would never preach again.

An eyewitness recorded, "The cries and shrieks at this period were truly terrific.... They pressed on, treading furiously over the dead and dying, tearing frantically at each other." Spurgeon nearly lost consciousness. He was rushed from the platform and "taken home more dead than alive." After the crowds dissipated, seven corpses were lying in the grass. Twenty-eight people were seriously injured.

The depression that resulted from this disaster left Spurgeon prostrate for days. "Even the sight of the Bible brought from me a flood of tears and utter distraction of mind." The newspapers added to his emotional deterioration. "Mr. Spurgeon is a preacher who hurls damnation at the heads of his sinful hearers…a ranting charlatan." By all accounts, it looked as if his ministry was over. "It might well seem that the ministry which promised to be so largely influential," Spurgeon said, "was silenced for ever."

When Spurgeon ascended the pulpit on November 2, two weeks later, he opened with a prayer. "We are assembled here, O Lord, this day, with mingled feelings of joy and sorrow.… Thy servant feared that he should never be able to meet this congregation again."

Although he would never fully recover from this disaster and grew anxious when preaching to large crowds, Spurgeon's ministry did not end on October 19, 1856. He later said, "I have gone to the very bottoms of the mountains, as some of you know, in a night that never can be erased from my memory…but, as far as my witness goes, I can say that the Lord is able to save unto the uttermost and in the last extremity, and He has been a good God to me."

The joy that Spurgeon exemplified even in difficult circumstances was based not only his own ability to recover, but on God's ability to replenish. It was a joy that balmed Spurgeon in future controversies when friends betrayed him, students disowned him, and family opposed him. The same God who called Spurgeon to London to preach his Word would not abandon him on the banks of the Thames. On the contrary, God used this horrible event in Spurgeon's life to save the lives of countless others, for the widely circulated negative press put the young pastor on England's radar – and eventually on the world's.

Spurgeon possessed a radical joy – a joy rooted in the soil of the supremacy of the God who was great and grand enough to make good things come out of evil. As Joseph told his brothers, "You intended to harm me, but God intended it for good to accomplish what is now being done, the saving of many lives" (Gen. 50:20). Spurgeon confessed,

> I bear my witness that the worst days I have ever had have turned out to be my best days. And when God has seemed most cruel to me, he has then been most kind. If there is anything in this world for which I would bless him more than for anything else, it is for pain and affliction. I am sure that in these things the richest, tenderest love has been manifested to me. Our Father's wagons rumble most heavily when they are bringing us the richest freight of the bullion of his grace. Love letters from heaven are often sent in black-edged envelopes. The cloud that is black with horror is big with mercy. Fear not the storm. It brings healing in its wings, and when Jesus is with you in the vessel, the tempest only hastens the ship to its desired haven.

The sermons in this book testify to the goodness and grace of God in Spurgeon's life. Their words were forged in the mind of a man who knew well the anvil of affliction. These six sermons stand as a reminder that God's people must endure the sorrow of suffering, and yet, joy comes in the morning (Ps. 30:5).

Spurgeon is here at his very best. Granted, his insights can be unpredictable and unconventional. Spurgeon pulls wisdom from unexpected places. But his words never fail to profit the eager listener. And if you follow them, you will inevitably find yourself standing in the presence of the Christ who uses suffering to hammer his people into holiness and purify them as gold.

The weight of Spurgeon's sermons is felt not in the creation of a new theology, but instead in the recasting of a very old one. It is as though Spurgeon shines a light through the prism of his passage until the reader is bathed in a kaleidoscope of truth. Be careful not to blink, lest you miss a blessing.

"I want you to see not only the sparkling fountain of joy," writes Spurgeon, "but to drink deep draughts of it; yes, and drink all the week, and all the month, and all the year, and all the rest of your lives, both in time and in eternity."

Christian T. George,
Assistant Professor of Historical Theology and Curator of the Spurgeon Library
Midwestern Baptist Theological Seminary, Kansas City, Missouri

1
Joy, a Duty

'Rejoice in the Lord alway: and again I say, Rejoice'.
(Phil. 4:4)

There is a marvellous medicinal power in joy. Most medicines are distasteful; but this, which is the best of all medicines, is sweet to the taste, and comforting to the heart. We noticed, in our reading, that there had been a little tiff between two sisters in the church at Philippi – I am glad that we do not know what the quarrel was about; I am usually thankful for ignorance on such subjects – but, as a cure for disagreements, the apostle says, 'Rejoice in the Lord alway.' People who are very happy, especially those who are very happy in the Lord, are not apt either to give offence or to take offence. Their minds are so sweetly occupied with higher things, that they are not easily distracted by the little troubles which naturally arise among such imperfect creatures as we are. Joy in the Lord is the cure for all discord. Should it not be so? What is this joy but the concord of the soul, the accord of the heart, with the joy of heaven? Joy in the Lord, then, drives away the discords of earth.

Further, brethren, notice that the apostle, after he had said, 'Rejoice in the Lord alway,' commanded the Philippians to be careful [anxious] for nothing, thus implying that joy in the Lord is one of the best preparations for the trials of this life. The cure for care is joy in the Lord. No, my brother, you will not be able to keep on with your fretfulness; no, my sister, you will not be able to weary yourself any longer with your anxieties, if the Lord will but fill you with His joy. Then, being satisfied with your God, yea, more than satisfied, overflowing with delight in Him, you will say to yourself, 'Why art thou cast down, O my soul? And why art thou disquieted in me? Hope thou in God: for I shall yet praise him for the help of his countenance.'

What is there on earth that is worth fretting for even for five minutes? If one could gain an imperial crown by a day of care, it would be too great an expense for a thing which would bring more care with it. Therefore, let us be thankful, let us be joyful in the Lord. I count it one of the wisest things that, by rejoicing in the Lord, we commence our heaven here below. It is possible so to do, it is profitable so to do, and we are commanded so to do. Now I come to the text itself, 'Rejoice in the Lord alway; and again I say, Rejoice.'

It will be our first business at this time to consider **The Grace Commanded**, this grace of joy; 'Rejoice in the Lord,' says the apostle. In the first place, *this is a very delightful thing*. What a gracious God we serve, who makes delight to be a duty, and who commands us to rejoice! Should we not at once be obedient to such a command as this? It is intended that we should be happy. That is the meaning of the precept, that we should be cheerful; more than that, that we should be thankful; more than that, that we should rejoice. I think this word 'rejoice' is almost a French word; it is not only joy, but it is joy over again, re-joice. You know, *re* usually signifies the re-duplication of a thing, the taking it over again. We are to joy, and then we are to re-joy. We are to chew the cud of delight; we are to roll the dainty morsel under our tongue till we get the very essence out of it. 'Rejoice.' Joy is a delightful thing. You cannot be too happy, brother. Nay, do not suspect yourself of being wrong because you are full of delight. You know it is said of the divine wisdom, 'Her ways are ways of pleasantness, and all her paths are peace.' Provided that it is joy in the Lord, you cannot have too much of it. The fly is drowned in the honey, or the sweet syrup into which he plunges himself; but this heavenly syrup of delight will not drown your soul, or intoxicate your heart. It will do you good, and not evil, all the days of your life. God never commanded us to do a thing which would really harm us; and when He bids us rejoice, we may be sure that this is as delightful as it is safe, and as safe as it is delightful. Come, brothers and sisters, I am inviting you now to no distasteful duty when, in the name of my Master, I say to you, as Paul said to the Philippians under the teaching of the Holy Spirit, 'Rejoice in the Lord alway: and again I say, Rejoice.'

But, next, *this is a demonstrative duty:* 'Rejoice in the Lord.' There may be such a thing as a dumb joy, but I hardly think that it can keep dumb long. Joy! joy! Why, it speaks for itself! It is like a candle lighted in a dark chamber; you need not sound a trumpet, and say, 'Now light has come.' The candle proclaims itself by its own brilliance; and when joy comes into a man, it shines out of his eyes, it sparkles in his countenance. There is a something about every limb of the man that betokens that his body, like a well-tuned harp, has had its strings put in order. Joy – it refreshes the marrow of the bones; it quickens the flowing of the blood in the veins; it is a healthy thing in all respects. It is a speaking thing, a demonstrative thing; and I am sure that joy in the Lord ought to have a tongue. When the Lord sends you affliction, sister, you generally grumble loudly enough; when the Lord tries you, my dear brother, you generally speak fast enough about that. Now when, on the other hand, the Lord multiplies His mercies to you, do speak about it, do sing about it. I cannot recollect, since I was a boy, ever seeing in the newspapers columns of thankfulness and expressions of delight about the prosperity of business in England. It is a long, long time since I was first able to read newspapers – a great many years now; but I do not recollect the paragraphs in which it was said that everybody was getting on in the world, and growing rich; but as soon as there was any depression in business, what lugubrious articles appeared concerning the dreadful times which had fallen upon the agricultural interest and every other interest! Oh, my dear brethren, from the way some of you grumble, I might imagine you were all ruined if I did not know better! I knew some of you when you were not worth two pence, and you are pretty well-to-do now; you have got on uncommonly well for men who are being ruined! From the way some people talk, you might imagine that everybody is bankrupt, and that we are all going to the dogs together; but it is not so, and what a pity it is that we do not give the Lord some of our praises when we have better times! If we are so loud and so eloquent over our present woes, why could we not have been as eloquent and as loud in thanksgiving for the blessings that God formerly vouchsafed to us? Perhaps the mercies buried in oblivion have been to heaven, and accused us to the Lord, and therefore He has sent us the sorrows of today. True joy, when it is joy in the Lord, must speak; it cannot hold its tongue, it must praise the name of the Lord.

Further, *this blessed grace of joy is very contagious.* It is a great privilege, I think, to meet a truly happy man, a graciously happy man. My mind goes back at this moment to that dear man of God who used to be with us, years ago, whom we called 'Old Father Dransfield'. What a lump of sunshine that man was! I think that I never came into this place, with a heavy heart, but the very sight of him seemed to fill me with exhilaration, for his joy was wholly in his God! An old man and full of years, but as full of happiness as he was full of days; always having something to tell you to encourage you. He constantly made a discovery of some fresh mercy for which we were again to praise God. O dear brethren, let us rejoice in the Lord, that we may set others rejoicing! One dolorous spirit brings a kind of plague into the house; one person who is always wretched seems to stop all the birds singing wherever he goes; but, as the birds pipe to each other, and one morning songster quickens all the rest, and sets the groves ringing with harmony, so will it be with the happy cheerful spirit of a man who obeys the command of the text, 'Rejoice in the Lord alway.' This grace of joy is contagious.

Besides, dear brethren, *joy in the Lord is influential for good.* I am sure that there is a mighty influence wielded by a consistently joyous spirit. See how little children are affected by the presence of a happy person. There is much more in the tone of the life than there is in the particular fashion of the life. It may be the life of one who is very poor, but oh, how poverty is gilded by a cheerful spirit! It may be the life of one who is well read and deeply instructed; but, oh, if there be a beauty of holiness, and a beauty of happiness added to the learning, nobody talks about 'the blue stocking' or 'the book-worm' being dull and heavy. Oh, no, there is a charm about holy joy! I wish we had more of it! There are many more flies caught with honey than with vinegar; and there are many more sinners brought to Christ by happy Christians than by doleful Christians. Let us sing unto the Lord as long as we live; and, mayhap, some weary sinner, who has discovered the emptiness of sinful pleasure, will say to himself, 'Why, after all, there must be something real about the joy of these Christians; let me go and learn how I may have it.' And when he comes and sees it in the light of your gladsome countenance, he will be likely to learn it, God helping him, so as never to forget it. 'Rejoice in the Lord alway,' says the apostle, for joy is a most influential grace, and every child of God ought to possess it in a high degree.

I want you to notice, dear friends, that *this rejoicing is commanded.* It is not a matter that is left to your option; it is not set before you as a desirable thing which you can do without, but it is a positive precept of the Holy Spirit to all who are in the Lord: 'Rejoice in the Lord alway.' We ought to obey this precept because joy in the Lord makes us like God. He is the happy God; ineffable bliss is the atmosphere in which He lives, and He would have His people to be happy. Let the devotees of Baal cut themselves with knives and lancets, and make hideous outcries if they will; but the servants of Jehovah must not even mar the corners of their beard. Even if they fast, they shall anoint their head, and wash their face, that they appear not unto men to fast, for a joyous God desires a joyous people.

You are commanded to rejoice, brethren, because this is for your profit. Holy joy will oil the wheels of your life's machinery. Holy joy will strengthen you for your daily labour. Holy joy will beautify you, and, as I have already said, give you an influence over the lives of others. It is upon this point that I would most of all insist, we are commanded to rejoice in the Lord. If you cannot speak the gospel, live the gospel by your cheerfulness; for what is the gospel? Glad tidings of great joy; and you who believe it must show by its effect upon you that it is glad tidings of great joy to you. I do believe that a man of God – under trial and difficulty and affliction, bearing up, and patiently submitting with holy acquiescence, and still rejoicing in God – is a real preacher of the gospel, preaching with an eloquence which is mightier than words can ever be, and which will find its secret and silent way into the hearts of those who might have resisted other arguments. Oh, do, then, listen to the text, for it is a command from God, 'Rejoice in the Lord alway!'

May I just pause here, and hand this commandment round to all of you who are members of this church, and to all of you who are truly members of Christ? You are bidden to rejoice in the Lord alway; you are not allowed to sit there, and fret, and fume; you are not permitted to complain and groan. Mourner, you are commanded to put on beauty for ashes, and the oil of joy for mourning. For this purpose your Saviour came, the Spirit of the Lord is upon Him for this very end, that He might make you to rejoice. Therefore, sing with the prophet, 'I will greatly rejoice in the Lord, my soul shall be joyful in my God; for he hath clothed me with the garments of salvation, he hath covered me with a robe of righteousness, as a bridegroom decketh himself with ornaments, and as a bride adorneth herself with her jewels.'

Now we come to the second head, on which I will speak but briefly; that is, **The Joy Discriminated**: 'Rejoice *in the Lord.*' Notice *the sphere of this joy:* 'Rejoice in the Lord.' We read in Scripture that children are to obey their parents 'in the Lord'. We read of men and women being married 'only in the Lord'. Now, dear friends, no child of God must go outside that ring, 'in the Lord'. There is where you are, where you ought to be, where you must be. You cannot truly rejoice if you get outside that ring; therefore, see that you do nothing which you cannot do 'in the Lord'. Mind that you seek no joy which is not joy in the Lord; if you go after the poisonous sweets of this world, woe be to you. Never rejoice in that which is sinful, for all such rejoicing is evil. Flee from it; it can do you no good. That joy which you cannot share with God is not a right joy for you. No; 'in the Lord' is the sphere of your joy.

But I think that the apostle also means that *God is to be the great object of your joy:* 'Rejoice in the Lord.' Rejoice in the Father, your Father who is in heaven, your loving, tender, unchangeable God. Rejoice, too, in the Son, your Redeemer, your Brother, the Husband of your soul, your Prophet, Priest, and King. Rejoice also in the Holy Ghost, your Quickener, your Comforter, in Him who shall abide with you for ever. Rejoice in the one God of Abraham, of Isaac, and of Jacob; in Him delight yourselves, as it is written, 'Delight thyself also in the Lord; and he shall give thee the desires of thine heart.' We cannot have too much of this joy in the Lord, for the great Jehovah is our exceeding joy.

Or if, by 'the Lord' is meant the Lord Jesus, then let me invite, persuade, command you to delight in the Lord Jesus, incarnate in your flesh, dead for your sins, risen for your justification, gone into the glory claiming victory for you, sitting at the right hand of God interceding for you, reigning over all worlds on your behalf, and soon to come to take you up into His glory that you may be with Him for ever. Rejoice in the Lord Jesus. This is a sea of delight; blessed are they that dive into its utmost depths. Sometimes, brethren and sisters, you cannot rejoice in anything else, but you can rejoice in the Lord; then, rejoice in Him to the full. Do not rejoice in your temporal prosperity, for riches take to themselves wings, and fly away. Do not rejoice even in your great successes in the work of God. Remember how the seventy disciples came back to Jesus, and said, 'Lord, even the devils are subject unto us through thy name,' and He answered, 'Notwithstanding in this rejoice not, that the spirits are subject unto you; but rather rejoice, because your names are written in heaven.' Do not rejoice in your privileges; I mean, do not make the great joy of your life to be the fact that you are favoured with this and that external privilege or ordinance, but rejoice in God. He changes not. If the Lord be your joy, your joy will never dry up. All other things are but for a season; but God is for ever and ever. Make Him your joy, the whole of your joy, and then let this joy absorb your every thought. Be baptized into this joy; plunge into the deeps of this unutterable bliss of joy in God.

Thirdly, let us think of **The Time Appointed** for this rejoicing: 'Rejoice in the Lord alway.'

'Alway.' Well, then, that begins at once, certainly; so let us now begin to rejoice in the Lord. If any of you have taken a gloomy view of religion, I beseech you to throw that gloomy view away at once. 'Rejoice in the Lord alway,' therefore, rejoice in the Lord now. I recollect what a damper I had, as a young Christian, when I had but lately believed in Jesus Christ. I felt that, as the Lord had said, 'He that believeth in me hath everlasting life,' I, having believed in Him, had everlasting life, and I said so, with the greatest joy and delight and enthusiasm, to an old Christian man. And he said to me, 'Beware of presumption! There are a great many who think they have eternal life, but who have not got it,' which was quite true; but, for all that, is there not more presumption in doubting God's promise than there is in believing it? Is there any presumption in taking God at His word?

Is there not gross presumption in hesitating and questioning as to whether these things are so or not? If God says that they are so, then they are so, whether I feel that they are so or not; and it is my place, as a believer, to accept God's bare word, and rest on it. 'We count cheques as cash,' said one who was making up accounts. Good cheques are to be counted as cash, and the promises of God, though as yet unfulfilled, are as good as the blessings themselves, for God cannot lie, or make a promise that He will not perform. Let us, therefore, not be afraid of being glad, but begin to be glad at once if we have hitherto taken a gloomy view of true religion, and have been afraid to rejoice.

When are we to be glad? 'Rejoice in the Lord alway;' that is, *when you cannot rejoice in anything or anyone but God.* When the fig-tree does not blossom, when there is no fruit on the vine and no herd in the stall, when everything withers and decays and perishes, when the worm at the root of the gourd has made it to die, then rejoice in the Lord. When the day darkens into evening, and the evening into midnight, and the midnight into a sevenfold horror of great darkness, rejoice in the Lord; and when that darkness does not clear, but becomes more dense and Egyptian, when night succeedeth night, and neither sun nor moon nor stars appear, still rejoice in the Lord alway. He who uttered these words had been a night and a day in the deep, he had been stoned, he had suffered from false brethren, he had been in peril of his life, and yet most fittingly do those lips cry out to us, 'Rejoice in the Lord alway.' Aye, at the stake itself have martyrs fulfilled this word; they clapped their hands amid the fire that was consuming them. Therefore, rejoice in the Lord when you cannot rejoice in any other.

But also take care that you *rejoice in the Lord when you have other things to rejoice in.* When He loads your table with good things, and your cup is overflowing with blessings, rejoice in *Him* more than in *them.* Forget not that the Lord your Shepherd is better than the green pastures and the still waters, and rejoice not in the pastures or in the waters in comparison with your joy in the Shepherd who gives you all. Let us never make gods out of our goods; let us never allow what God gives us to supplant the Giver. Shall the wife love the jewels that her husband gave her better than she loves him who gave them to her? That were an evil love, or no love at all. So, let us love God first, and rejoice in the Lord alway when the day is brightest, and multiplied are the other joys that He permits us to have.

'Rejoice in the Lord alway.' That is, *if you have not rejoiced before, begin to do so at once*; and *when you have long rejoiced, keep on at it.* I have known, sometimes, that things have gone so smoothly that I have said, 'There will be a check to this prosperity; I know that there will. Things cannot go on quite so pleasantly always.'

> More the treacherous calm I dread
> Than tempests lowering overhead.

One is apt to spoil his joy by the apprehension that there is some evil coming. Now listen to this: 'He shall not be afraid of evil tidings: his heart is fixed, trusting in the Lord.' 'Rejoice in the Lord alway.' Do not anticipate trouble. 'Sufficient unto the day is the evil thereof.' Take the good that God provides thee, and rejoice not merely in it, but in Him who provided it. So mayest thou enjoy it without fear, for there is good salt with that food which is eaten as coming from the hand of God.

'Rejoice in the Lord alway.' That is, *when you get into company, then rejoice in the Lord.* Do not be ashamed to let others see that you are glad. *Rejoice in the Lord also when you are alone;* I know what happens to some of you on Sunday night. You have had such a blessed Sabbath, and you have gone away from the Lord's Table with the very flavour of heaven in your mouths; and then some of you have had to go home where everything is against you. The husband does not receive you with any sympathy with your joy, or the father does not welcome you with any fellowship in your delight. Well, but still, 'Rejoice in the Lord *alway.*' When you cannot get anybody else to rejoice with you, still continue to rejoice. There is a way of looking at everything which will show you that the blackest cloud has a silver lining. There is a way of looking at all things in the light of God, which will turn into sweetness that which otherwise had been bitter as gall.

I do not know whether any of you keep a quassia cup at home. If you do, you know that it is made of wood, and you pour water into the bowl, and the water turns bitter directly before you drink it. You may keep this cup as long as you like, but it always embitters the water that is put into it. I think that I know some dear brethren and sisters who always seem to have one of these cups handy. Now, instead of that, I want you to buy a cup of another kind that shall make everything sweet, whatever it is. Whatever God pleases to pour out of the bowl of providence shall come into your cup, and your contentment, your delight in God, shall sweeten it all. God bless you, dear friends, with much of this holy joy!

So now I finish with the fourth head, which is this, **the emphasis laid on the command**: 'Rejoice in the Lord alway: *and again I say, Rejoice.*' What does that mean, 'Again I say, Rejoice?' This was, first, *to show Paul's love* *for the Philippians.* He wanted them to be happy. They had been so kind to him, and they had made him so happy, that he said, 'Oh, dear brethren, do rejoice; dear sisters, do rejoice. I say it twice over to you, "Be happy, be happy," because I love you so well that I am anxious to have you beyond all things else to rejoice in the Lord alway.'

I also think that, perhaps, he said it twice over to suggest the *difficulty of continual joy.* It is not so easy as some think always to rejoice. It may be for you young people, who are yet strong in limb, who have few aches and pains, and none of the infirmities of life. It may be an easy thing to those placed in easy circumstances, with few cares and difficulties; but there are some of God's people who need great grace if they are to rejoice in the Lord always; and the apostle knew that, so he said, 'Again I say, Rejoice.' He repeats the precept, as much as to say, 'I know it is a difficult thing, and so I the more earnestly press it upon you. Again I say, Rejoice.'

I think, too, that he said it twice over, *to assert the possibility of it.* This was as much as if he had said, 'I told you to rejoice in the Lord always. You opened your eyes, and looked with astonishment upon me; but, "Again I say, Rejoice." It is possible, it is practicable; I have not spoken unwisely. I have not told you to do what you never can do; but with deliberation I write it down, "Again I say, Rejoice." You can be happy. God the Holy Ghost can lift you above the down-draggings of the flesh, and of the world, and of the devil; and you may be enabled to live upon the mount of God beneath the shinings of His face. "Again I say, Rejoice."'

Do you not think that this was intended also *to impress upon them the importance of the duty*? '*Again* I say, Rejoice.'

Some of you will go and say, 'I do not think that it matters much whether I am happy or not, I shall get to heaven, however gloomy I am, if I am sincere.' 'No,' says Paul, 'that kind of talk will not do; I cannot have you speak like that. Come, I must have you rejoice, I do really conceive it to be a Christian's bounden duty, and so, "*Again*, I say, Rejoice."'

But do you not think, also, that Paul repeated the command *to allow of special personal testimony*? '*Again*, I say, Rejoice. I, Paul, a sufferer to the utmost extent for Christ's sake, even now an ambassador in bonds, shut up in a dungeon, I say to you, Rejoice.' Paul was a greatly-tried man, but he was a blessedly happy man. There is not one of us but would gladly change conditions with Paul, if that were possible, now that we see the whole of his life written out; and tonight, looking across the ages, over all the scenes of trouble which he encountered, he says to us, 'Brethren, rejoice in the Lord alway: and again I say, Rejoice.'

Did you ever notice how full of joy this Epistle to the Philippians is? Will you spare me just a minute while I get you to run your eye through it, to observe what a joyful letter it is? You notice that, in the first chapter, Paul gets only as far as the fourth verse when he says, 'Always in every prayer of mine for you all making request with joy.' Now he is in his right vein; he is so glad because of what God has done for the Philippians that, when he prays for them, he mixes joy with his prayer. In the eighteenth verse, he declares that he found joy even in the opposition of those who preached Christ in order to rival him. Hear what he says: 'The one preach Christ of contention, not sincerely, supposing to add affliction to my bonds: but the other of love, knowing that I am set for the defence of the gospel. What then? Notwithstanding, every way, whether in pretence, or in truth, Christ is preached; and I therein do rejoice, yea, and will rejoice.' And he does not finish the chapter till, in the twenty-fifth verse, he declares that he had joy even in the expectation of not going to heaven just yet, but living a little longer to do good to these people: 'And having this confidence, I know that I shall abide and continue with you all for your furtherance and joy of faith; that your rejoicing may be more abundant in Jesus Christ for me by my coming to you again.' You see it is joy, joy, joy, joy. Paul seems to go from stave to stave of the ladder of light, as if he were climbing up from Nero's dungeon into heaven itself by way of continual joy. So he writes, in the second verse of the second chapter, 'Fulfil ye my joy, that ye be likeminded, having the same love, being of one accord, of one mind.'

When he gets to the sixteenth verse, he says, 'That I may rejoice in the day of Christ, that I have not run in vain, neither laboured in vain.' But I am afraid that I should weary you if I went through the Epistle thus, slowly, verse by verse. Just notice how he begins the third chapter: 'Finally, my brethren, rejoice in the Lord.' The word is sometimes rendered 'farewell'. When he says, 'Rejoice,' it is the counterpart of 'welcome'. We say to a man who comes to our house, 'Salve,' 'Welcome.' When he goes away, it is our duty to 'speed the parting guest', and say, 'Farewell.' This is what Paul meant to say here. 'Finally, my brethren, fare you well in the Lord. Be happy in the Lord. Rejoice in the Lord.' And I do not think that I can finish up my sermon better than by saying on this Sabbath night, 'Finally, my brethren, fare you well, be happy in the Lord.'

> Fare thee well! and if for ever,
> Still for ever, fare thee well.

May that be your position, so to walk with God that your fare shall be that of angels! May you eat angels' food, the manna of God's love! May your drink be from the rock that flows with a pure stream! So may you feed and so may you drink until you come unto the mount of God, where you shall see His face unveiled, and standing in His exceeding brightness, shall know His glory, being glorified with the saved. Till then, be happy. Why, even, 'the thought of such amazing bliss should constant joys create.' Be happy. If the present be dreary, it will soon be over. Oh, but a little while, and we shall be transferred from these seats below to the thrones above! We shall go from the place of aching brows to the place where they all wear crowns, from the place of weary hands to where they bear the palm branch of victory, from the place of mistake and error and sin, and consequent grief, to the place where they are without fault before the throne of God, for they have washed their robes, and made them white in the blood of the Lamb. Come, then, let us make a solemn league and covenant together in the name of God, and let it be called 'The Guild of the Happy'; for the 'Favourites of the Heavenly King may speak their joys abroad'. Nay, they *must* speak their joys abroad; let us endeavour to do so always, by the help of the Holy Spirit. Amen and Amen.

2

The Joy of Jesus

'In that hour Jesus rejoiced in spirit, and said,
I thank thee, O Father, Lord of heaven and earth,
that thou hast hid these things from the wise and
prudent, and hast revealed them unto babes: even
so, Father; for so it seemed good in thy sight. All
things are delivered to me of my Father: and no
man knoweth who the Son is, but the Father; and
who the Father is, but the Son, and he to whom
the Son will reveal him.'
(Luke 10:21, 22)

Last Lord's-day morning we considered the lamentations of Jesus; we will now turn our thoughts to the joys of Jesus. It is remarkable that this is the only instance on record in the Gospels in which our Lord is said to have rejoiced. It stands alone, and is, therefore, the more to be prized: 'In that hour Jesus rejoiced in spirit.' He was the 'man of sorrows and acquainted with grief' for our sakes, and therefore we are not astonished to find few indications of joy in the story of His life. Yet I do not think it would be fair to infer from the fact of a solitary mention of His rejoicing that He did not rejoice at other times; on the contrary, our Lord must, despite His sorrow, have possessed a peaceful, happy spirit. He was infinitely benevolent, and went about doing good; and benevolence always finds a quiet delight in blessing others. The joy of the lame when they leaped, and of the blind when they saw, must have gladdened the soul of Jesus. To cause happiness to others must bring home to a sympathetic bosom some degree of pleasure. Sir Philip Sydney was wont to say, 'Doing good is the only certainly happy action of a man's life;' and assuredly it is hard to see how the love of Jesus could refrain from rejoicing in blessing those around Him.

Moreover, our Lord was so pure that He had a well of joy within which could not fail Him. If it be indeed true that virtue is true happiness, then Jesus of Nazareth was happy. The poet said,

> What nothing earthly gives, or can destroy,
> The soul's calm sunshine and the heartfelt joy,
> Is virtue's prize.

Such calm and joy must have been the Saviour's, though for our sake He bowed beneath the heavy load of sorrow. The perfectly holy God is the perfectly happy God; and the perfectly holy Christ, had it not been that He had taken upon Himself our griefs and sicknesses, would have been perfectly happy; but even with our griefs and sicknesses there must have been a deep peace of soul within Him which sustained Him in His deepest woe. Did not the Father Himself say of His beloved Son, 'Thou lovest righteousness, and hatest wickedness: therefore God, thy God, hath anointed thee with the oil of gladness above thy fellows'?

Nor is this all, for our blessed Lord lived in unbroken fellowship with the Father, and fellowship with God will not permit a soul to abide in darkness: for, walking with God, he walks in the light as God is in the light. Such a mind may, for certain purposes, come under clouds and glooms; but light is sown for the righteous, and it will speedily break forth as the dawn of day. Those nights of prayer and days of perfect service must have brought their own calm to the tried heart of the Son of God.

Besides, Christ Jesus was a man of faith; faith's highest exposition and example. He is 'the author and the finisher of faith,' in whom we see its life, walk, and triumph. Our Lord was the incarnation of perfect confidence in the Father: in His life all the histories of great believers are summed up. Read the eleventh of the Hebrews, and see the great cloud of witnesses, and then mark how in the twelfth chapter Paul bids us look to Jesus as though in His person the whole multitude of the witnesses could be seen. He it was, who 'for the joy that was set before him endured the cross, despising the shame.' His faith must, therefore, have anticipated the reward of His passion, and have brought the joy thereof home to him even while he sorrowed here. His joy was a light from the lamps of the future, which were to be kindled by His death and victory. He had meat to eat that His disciples knew not of; for His long-sighted eye saw further than they, and while they mourned His departure He saw the expediency of it, and told them that if they loved Him they would rejoice, because He was going to the Father.

Be sure of this, that our Lord felt beneath the great waterfloods of outward affliction an under-current of joy, for He said, 'These things have I spoken unto you, that my joy might remain in you, and that your joy might be full.' What meant He by this if He had no joy in His people? Could He have spoken so many happy words, and so often have said to His disciples, 'Be of good cheer,' if He had been always downcast Himself?

But still it is remarkable that our text should be the sole recorded instance of His joy, so far as the evangelists are concerned. It is clear that joy was not a distinguishing feature in our Lord's life, so as to strike the beholder. Peace may have sat serenely on His brow, but nothing of the exuberant spirits which are seen in some men, for His countenance was marred with lines of care and grief. We do not hear that He laughed, though it is thrice recorded that He wept; and here for once, as quite unique, we find the inspired assurance that He rejoiced. Because of its singularity the record deserves to be looked into with care that we may see the cause of delight so unusual.

The words here used are very emphatic. 'He rejoiced.' The Greek word is much stronger than the English rendering; it signifies 'to leap for joy'. It is the word of the blessed Virgin's song, 'My spirit hath rejoiced in God my Saviour.' Strong emotions of delight were visible upon our Lord's face, and were expressed by the tones of His voice as well as by His words. It is clear that He was greatly glad. The text also says, He 'rejoiced in spirit': that is, deep down in the very centre of His nature, in that largest and most capacious part of His human being, the Redeemer rejoiced. Man is body, soul, and spirit; but the spirit is the nobler and most vital part, and it was with a spiritual, inward, and most living joy that the Lord Jesus Christ rejoiced. It was joy of the truest and fullest sort which made the Saviour's heart to dance. Come we, then, near to this rejoicing Saviour, who wraps the garments of praise about Him, perfumed with delight; and let us see if we cannot learn somewhat from His joys, since, I trust, we gathered something from His griefs.

First, let us look at our Lord and note that His joy was **Joy in the Father's Revelation of the Gospel**. 'I thank thee, O Father, that thou hast hid these things from the wise and prudent, and hast revealed them unto babes.' He rejoices in His Father's revelation of the gospel. It was not joy in the fame which had gathered about His name insomuch that John heard of it in prison. It was not joy in the manifest tokens of power that went forth with His commissioners, though they rejoiced that devils were subject unto them; but it was joy in God's revealing the gospel to the sons of men.

I call your attention to the fact that He ascribed all that was done to the Father, and joyed that the Father was working with Him. His disciples came back to Him and said, 'Even the devils are subject unto us through thy Name'; and they spake not amiss, for the name of Jesus was their strength, and deserved honour; but the Lord, with that sacred self-abnegation which was so natural to Him, replies, 'I thank thee, O Father, that thou hast revealed these things.' He takes no honour unto Himself, but ascribes the glory unto the Father, who wrought with Him. Imitate Him, O ye who call Him Lord! Let the work of the Father be your joy. If God gives us any success in the preaching of the gospel let our joy be that the Father's power is going forth with the word. We are not so much to joy in our instrumentality as in the hand which uses the instrument, and works by it. Oh, misery! misery! to be attempting gospel ministry without God! But oh, bliss, bliss unspeakable, to feel that when we lift our hand God's hand is lifted too, and when we speak the word the voice of God is ringing through our feeble speech, and reaching the hearts of men! It is to true believers a great joy that the Father is bringing home His wandering children, and receiving penitents into His bosom.

The Saviour's joy was that through the Father's grace men were being enlightened. The seventy disciples had been from city to city, working miracles and preaching the gospel, and their Master was glad when they returned with tidings of success: 'In that hour Jesus rejoiced in spirit.' It pleases Jesus when the gospel has free course, and God is glorified thereby. Then, in measure, He sees of the travail of His soul, and is filled with satisfaction. Shall we not find our joy where He finds His? Shall we not enter into the joy of our Lord? Whenever we hear good news of a village evangelised, of a township moved by the glad tidings, of a country long shut up from the gospel at length opened to the word, let us feel our highest and deepest joy. Rather let us rejoice in this than in business prosperity or personal advantage. What if we can find no joy in our own circumstances, what if even spiritual affairs within our soul are full of difficulty; let us joy and rejoice that God the Father is revealing the light of His gospel among the sons of men. Be this our highest wish, 'Thy kingdom come,' and in that coming kingdom let us find our utmost happiness. Be sure that the joy which warmed the heart of Christ can do us no hurt: it must be a pure, sacred, and ennobling joy, and therefore let us indulge in it very largely. Christ's joy lay in the Father's sending forth His light and His truth, making men to see things which prophets and kings had desired to behold, but had not been favoured to see. Jesus rejoiced in this, that the blessings of grace were being revealed by the Father.

Further, our Saviour's joy lay very much in this, that this revelation to men was being made through such humble instruments. We read that 'he lifted up his eyes on his disciples, and said, Blessed be ye poor: for yours is the kingdom of God.' There was not among the twelve or the seventy, one person of any social status. They were the common people of the field and the sea. In after years Paul was raised up, a man richly endowed in learning, whose great abilities were used by the Lord, but the first ministers of Christ were a band of fishermen and countrymen, altogether unknown in the schools of learning, and regarded as 'unlearned and ignorant men'. The grandest era in the world's history was ushered in by nobodies: by persons who, like their leader, were despised and rejected of men. To any one of them it might have been said, 'For ye see your calling, brethren, how that not many wise men after the flesh, not many mighty, not many noble, are called: but God hath chosen the foolish things of the world to confound the wise, and God hath chosen the weak things of the world to confound the things which are mighty; and base things of the world, and things which are despised, hath God chosen, yea, and things which are not, to bring to nought things that are: that no flesh should glory in his presence.'

Observe carefully that the persons whom our Lord had been employing were not only obscure in origin, but they were of a low degree of spiritual understanding, were in fact babes in grace as well as worldly wisdom. Their joy, when they came back to tell what had been done, was evidently childish as well as gracious. They joyed in their success as children do in their little achievements; but their Lord was thankful, because He saw the open-heartedness and the simplicity of their characters in the gladsome way in which they cried, 'Lord, even the devils are subject to us through thy name,' and He thanked God that by such babes as these, such children, such true-hearted children, and yet such mere children, He was pleased to make known His word among the sons of men. Rest ye sure that our Lord even at this day finds a delight in the weakness of the instruments He uses.

> He takes the fool and makes him know
> The mysteries of his grace;
> To bring aspiring wisdom low,
> And all its pride abase.

Not you, ye scribes, who have counted every letter of the Old Testament, does He elect to be filled with the Spirit. Not you, ye Pharisees, who so abound in outward religion, does He choose to spread the inward life and light. Not you, ye Sadducees, who are versed in sceptical philosophy, and boast your cleverness, does He call to preach His gospel to the poor. He hath taken to be the heralds of His glory men from the Sea of Galilee whom ye despise: men, simple-hearted, ready to learn, and then as ready to tell out again, the message of salvation. Our Lord was by no means displeased with the absence of culture and learning in His followers, for the culture and learning of the period were utter vanity, but He was glad to see that they did not pretend to wisdom or astuteness, but came to Him in all simplicity to accept His teaching, because they believed Him to be the Son of God. Jesus rejoiced in spirit about this.

And yet, further, His great joy was that the converts were of such a character as they were. 'Thou hast hid these things from the wise and prudent, and hast revealed them unto babes.' It is true that certain persons sneeringly asked, 'Have any of the rulers or of the Pharisees believed in him?' There were some who thought lightly of Jesus because those whom they imagined to be learned men had not signified their adhesion to His cause; our Lord Himself had no concern in that direction, but called the Pharisees blind and the scribes hypocrites, as they assuredly were.

Other voices may have enquired, 'Who are these that follow Jesus? Of what class are His converts?' The answer would have been, 'They are rustics, fishermen, and common people, with here and there a woman of substance and a man of means. The bulk of them are the poor to whom for the first time the gospel is preached. Such have gathered to Christ and received His word.' Some even said that a parcel of boys and girls were in the streets crying, 'Hosanna,' and this showed how common-place the Preacher was.

At this day I have heard the Lord's people spoken of as a poor set; people of no position, a lot of persons whose names will never be known, a mere assembly of Jack, Tom, Harry, Mary, Susan, and the rest. This was the very thing to which Jesus refers with thankfulness. He was glad that He was surrounded by unsophisticated, childlike natures, rather than by Pharisees and scribes, who, even if they be converted, are sure to bring some of their old manners with them.

He was glad that the Father had revealed His light and His salvation to those who were lowly and humble, who, though poor in this world, were 'rich in faith, giving glory to God.' Thus you see that the very fact, which certain very superior people fling in our teeth as a disgrace, was to our Saviour a subject of joy. I have heard foolish ones sneer at certain churches which are earnest for the truth by affectedly asking, 'Who are they? A mob of common people, tradesmen or working men, and the like. Are there any of the aristocracy among them? Do you find any of the highly intellectual in their ranks?' What if we do not, we shall not therefore sorrow, but join with Jesus in saying, 'We thank thee, O Father, that thou hast hid these things from the wise and prudent, and hast revealed them unto babes.'

Christ found Himself at home among those open-hearted folks that gathered around Him, for He was Himself a child-man, who wore His heart upon His sleeve, boasting of no wisdom though He was wisdom's self. Our Lord never sought Himself, as the wise and prudent of His age did; but He was meek and lowly in heart, and therefore found Himself at home amongst a people who were willing to receive His teaching and eager to tell it out again to their countrymen; and so He blessed and praised God that such were chosen.

Oh, friends, it is not that Christ would not have the greatest come to Him, it is not that Christ would not have the learned come to Him; but so it is, that His greatest joy is that those come who, whatever the greatness or the littleness of their learning, are childlike in spirit, and like babes are willing to learn, and prepared to receive what He shall teach to them. He was glad to receive persons with lowly notions of their own intelligence, and a supreme belief in the veracity of their great Teacher.

If those who are reckoned to be learned profess to come to Christ they are generally a trial to the church. All the merely human learning that has ever come unto the church has, as a rule, been mischievous to it: and it always needs great grace to keep it in its right place. At first came the Gnostics with their philosophy, and into what perils they dragged the church of God I cannot stay to tell you: then arose others out of whose wisdom grew Arianism, and the church was well-nigh withered to her very heart by that deadly form of heresy. The schoolmen did for her much the same, and to this day whenever any of the would-be-thought-wise men meddle with religion, they tell us that the plain word of God, as we read it, must be interpreted by modern thought, and that it bears another meaning which only the cultured can possibly comprehend. When philosophy invades the domain of revelation it ends in perverting the gospel, and in bringing in 'another gospel which is not another'. It is with human wisdom as it is with human riches, how hardly shall they that have it enter into the kingdom of God!

True wisdom is another thing; that is a gift which cometh from above, and causeth no puffing up of the heart, for it adores the God from whom it came. The wisdom which is true and real the Lord is prepared to give to those who confess their unwisdom, to those who will be babes in His sight. It is not ignorance which God loves, but conceit that He hates. Knowledge is good, but the affectation of it is evil. O for more true wisdom! May God give us much of it, and may those who are babes as yet come to be men of full stature in Christ Jesus. Yet forget not your Lord's joy

in the character of His converts, but remember the lines
in which the poet of the sanctuary paraphrases our text:

> Jesus, the man of constant grief,
> A mourner all his days,
> His Spirit once rejoiced aloud,
> And turned his joy to praise.
>
> 'Father, I thank thy wondrous love,
> That hath revealed thy Son
> To men unlearned, and to babes
> Hath made thy gospel known.'
>
> 'The mysteries of redeeming grace
> Are hidden from the wise,
> While pride and carnal reasoning join
> To swell and blind their eyes.'

Our Lord's joy sprang from one other source, namely, His
view of the manner in which God was pleased to save His
people. It was by revealing these things to them. There
is, then, to every man who is saved a revelation, not of
anything over and above what is given us in the word of
God; but of that same truth to himself personally and with
power. In the word is the light; but what is needed is that
each man's eye should be opened by the finger of God to
see it. Truth in the Scriptures will never save till it becomes
truth in the heart: it must be 'revealed' unto the most
unprejudiced and true-hearted. Even men of childlike
spirits and receptive natures will not see the truth unless
it be specially revealed to them. There must be a work of
the Father through the Holy Ghost upon each intellect
and mind ere it can perceive the truth as it is in Jesus.

Hence, when unregenerate men tell us that they cannot see the beauty of the gospel, we are not at all astonished – we never thought they could; and when boastful men of 'culture' declare that the old-fashioned gospel is unworthy of the nineteenth century with all its enlightenment, we are not surprised; for we knew that they would think so. Blind men are little pleased with colour, and deaf men care little for music.

<u>Human wisdom cannot make a man without eyes see the light</u>. What do you know about the gospel, oh ye blinded wise men? What judges can you be of the light of revelation who seal up your eyes with the mud of your own cleverness, and then say you cannot see! Christ never intended that you should. He will only reveal Himself as He pleases, and He hath pleased to do this to another kind of persons from what you are. Oh, you that are wise in your own conceit, the gate of true wisdom is barred against you! You cannot by searching find out God, and when He graciously reveals Himself you refuse to see Him, and therefore it is just that you should perish in the dark. Well do you deserve this judgment. Let justice be done.

That God had been pleased to reveal Himself to many through the preaching of the seventy was a great joy to Jesus; and let us also rejoice whenever God reveals Himself to men. Let us be glad when one who is simple in heart is made a child by divine grace through being born again. Let us furthermore rejoice whenever conversion is wrought by instruments that cannot possibly claim the glory of it. Let us praise and bless God that salvation is His own work from first to last. Come, all ye who love the Father, and say, with the great Firstborn, 'I thank thee, O Father, Lord of heaven and earth, that thou hast hid these things from the wise and prudent, and hast revealed them unto babes: even so, Father; for so it seemed good in thy sight.'

I have thus tried, as far as I am able, to explain the cause of the Saviour's joy; I would now call your attention to **His Mode of Expressing That Joy**. I have noticed some kind of joy in conversions which has not been wise in its expression, but has savoured of glorying in the flesh. 'Oh, we have had a wonderful time, we have had a blessed season! We have been visited by those dear men, and we have exerted ourselves in downright earnest to get up a revival. We have done wonders.' Such talk will not do. Hear how the Saviour speaks; His joy finds tongue in thanksgiving, 'I thank thee, O Father.' He ascribes the work to the Father, and then renders all the praise to Him. This is the eloquence of joy – 'I thank thee, O Father.' Brethren, whenever you are happy, sing hymns of thanksgiving. 'Is any merry? Let him sing psalms.' The fittest language for joy, whether it be on earth or in heaven, is adoration and thanksgiving to God. Blessed be the name of the Lord that we are gladdened in the harvest field of Christian work; for it is He that giveth seed to the sower and causeth the word to spring up and bring forth fruit a hundred-fold.

Our Lord found expression for His joy in declaring the Father's sovereignty: 'I thank thee, O Father, Lord of heaven and earth.' Some shrink back from the idea of God as Lord of all things above and below. To them the free will of man seems the greatest of all facts; and lest there should be the slightest intrusion upon man's domain they would have God limited as to His absolute power. To magnify man they would minimise God. You will hear them talking against those of us who magnify divine sovereignty, and imputing to us the notion of a certain arbitrariness in God, although such a thought has never entered our minds. Jehovah, who gives no account of His matters, but orders all things according to the good pleasure of His will, is never arbitrary, unjust, or tyrannical: and yet He is absolute and uncontrolled, a sovereign who reigns by His own self-existent power, Himself the source and origin of all law. He can be trusted with absolute sovereignty, because He is infinite love and infinite goodness. I will go the utmost length as to the absolute supremacy of God, and His right to do as He wills, and especially to do as He wills with His own, which gospel grace most certainly is. He will have mercy on whom He will have mercy, and He will have compassion on whom He will have compassion. And none can stay His hand or say unto Him, What doest thou? When Christ was gladdest He expressed that gladness by ascribing unto God an infinite sovereignty, and shall that truth be gloomy to us? Nay, rather we will each one view the work of the Father's grace, and cry, 'I thank thee, O Father, and I thank thee all the more because I know that thou art Lord of heaven and earth.'

If I am addressing any who quarrel with the doctrine of the sovereignty of God, I would advise them to cease their rebellion, for 'the Lord reigneth.' Let them at least go as far as the Psalm, 'Let the people tremble'; even if they cannot go a little further and sing, 'The Lord reigneth; let the earth rejoice; let the multitude of isles be glad thereof.' Power and rule are best in the hands of the great Jehovah, who ever links together in His own single character both fatherhood and sovereignty. 'I thank thee, O Father, Lord of heaven and earth.' Dismiss from your minds all caricatures of the doctrine, and receive it in its purest form – 'the Lord is king for ever and ever. Hallelujah.' Your joy, if it be deeply spiritual and very great, will never find room enough for the sweep of its Atlantic waves, till you delight yourself in the absolute supremacy of God. The deep ground swell of delight within the Redeemer's soul could find no grander space over which it could expand its force than the unlimited power and dominion of the Lord of heaven and earth, whose key it is which opens or shuts the kingdom of heaven, whose word it is which hides or reveals the things of eternity.

Our Lord delighted in the special act of sovereignty which was before Him, that the Lord had 'hid these things from the wise and prudent, and had revealed them unto babes.' He communed with God in it, He took pleasure in it, and said, 'Even so, Father; for so it seemed good in thy sight.' His voice, as it were, went with the Father's voice; He agreed with the Father's choice, He rejoiced in it, He triumphed in it. The will of the Father was the will of Christ, and He had fellowship with the Father in every act of His sovereign choice; yea, He magnified God for it in His inmost spirit. He says, 'Even so, Father; for so it seemed good in thy sight;' for He knew that what seems good to God must be good. Some things seem good to us which are evil; but that which seemeth good to God is good. Jesus praises God about it for no other reason than it is God's good pleasure that it should be so.

Oh, what a state of heart it will be for you and me to get into when we can express our highest joy by a perfect acquiescence in the will of God, whatever that will may be. See here, brethren, the road to contentment, to peace, to happiness, yea, heavenly life this side the grave. If you ever come to feel that what pleases God pleases you, you will be glad even in affliction and tribulation. If your heart is ever schooled down to accept as your will that which is God's will, and to believe anything to be good because God thinks it good, then you may go through the rest of your days singing and waiting till your Lord takes you to His own bosom. Soon will you rise to the place where all the singers meet and sing for ever unto God and the Lamb; all self and rebellion being for ever banished.

Herein, then, Christ found a channel for His joy – in thanksgiving, in magnifying the divine sovereignty, in having communion with it and in delighting in it.

Thirdly, and briefly, I want you to see **Our Lord's Explanation of the Father's Act**. The Father had been pleased to hide these things from the wise and prudent and to reveal them unto babes, and Jesus Christ is perfectly satisfied with that order of things, quite content with the kind of converts He has and the kind of preachers that God has given Him.

For, first, the Lord Jesus does not need *prestige*. Read the twenty-second verse: 'All things are delivered to me of my Father.' A mere pretender, when he begins to prophesy and set himself up for a religious leader, how pleased he is when some learned doctor endorses his claims! If some man of wealth and station comes to his side how he plumes himself. The Saviour of our souls sought no such aids. The verdict of the world's literati could not make His word more truthful than it is, nor more convincing, for its power lies in the Spirit which reveals it. If great men say 'Aye,' they will not make His doctrine more sure; nor will they make it less truthful if they all say 'Nay.' Prestige for Christ! It is blasphemy to think of such a thing. 'All things,' saith He, 'are delivered to me of my Father.' High priests and leaders of religion denounce Him, but all things are delivered unto Him of His Father. The Sanhedrin determine to put Him down, but all things are delivered unto Him of the Father. The learned deride His claims to be the Messiah! What matters it to Christ? The Father has committed all things into His hand. He stands alone, and asks for no allies; His own power, unborrowed and unaided, is quite sufficient for His purposes. Do you think, brethren, that we are going to stay our preaching of the gospel until we shall have the so-called culture and intellect of the age upon our side to say, 'It is even so'? Not we, but rather do we believe God in the teeth of the wiseacres, and say, 'Let God be true, and every man a liar.' Jesus needs no imprimatur from scholars, no patronage from princes, no apologies from orators. The pomp, and power, and wisdom, and cunning of the world were not with Him, and He thanks God that He is not encumbered with such doubtful gain, but that this truth has been revealed to those who are not wise in their own eyes, nor intelligent in their own esteem, but, like children, willing to learn from God, and glad to believe all that He reveals.

See how the Lord explains it yet further, by showing that human wisdom cannot find out God. 'No man knoweth who the Son is but the Father, and who the Father is but the Son.' No man; though he be a master in Israel. Men of science may puzzle their brains, and with great ingenuity they may try to thread the intricacies of the unknown, but they must err from the truth if they refuse revelation. Such a thing as natural religion, spontaneously born of man's intellect, does not exist. 'Oh,' say you, 'surely there is much of it.' I say that whatever is truly religious in it was borrowed from revelation, and has been handed down by tradition. Talk of comparative religions – there is but one, and the other pretenders have stolen certain of its clothes. Men see, no doubt, much of God in nature, but they would not have done so had there been no revelation. First came the light through revelation, and then afterwards, when men saw it reflected from various objects, they dreamed that the light came out of the reflectors. Men hear something of revealed truth, and when their thoughts run in that line, that which they have heard is awakened in their minds, and they think themselves inventors. God is not known except as He reveals Himself, nor can He be discovered by human ingenuity. Carnal wit and thought tend not that way, but tend from God unto blackest darkness. God is only to be known through Christ, so the text saith: 'No man knoweth who the Father is but the Son, and he to whom the Son will reveal him.' As the light, after God had created it, was lodged in the sun, so is all knowledge of God treasured up in Christ as the Sun of righteousness. He it is that in Himself hath light, the light that lighteneth every man that cometh into the world, if he be lightened at all. We must receive Christ or abide in darkness; yea, and the light which is in Christ is not perceptible by any man except by revelation. What saith the text, 'No man knoweth who the Son is, but the Father; and who the Father is, but the Son, and he to whom the Son will reveal him'? There must be a special and distinct revelation of Christ, and of the Father by Christ to each man, or else he will remain in blindness to the day of his death.

The power, then, which lies in merely human wisdom is a force which often hinders men from coming under the influence of revelation. Only by revelation can they know, and by a revelation personally receive. But the man is so wise that he does not want to be taught, he can find it out for himself. Yield himself to an infallible book or an infallible spirit? Not he! Well, then, because of his very wisdom he becomes incapable of learning. Truth to tell, what is human wisdom? The supposed wisdom of man is folly, that is the short for it all. They write a history sometime of religious thought, and of the various phases through which Christianity has gone, and on this they ground remarks; but I should like somebody to write a truthful history of philosophy.

The history of philosophy is a record of the insanities of mankind: a catalogue of lunacies. You shall see one generation of philosophers busily engaged in refuting those that went before them, and doing it very well indeed. But what will the next generation do? Why refute this! The philosophies that were current one hundred years ago are all exploded now, and all the teachings of today, except such as are clear matters of fact, will be exploded ere I go down to my grave, if I live to be grey-headed. There is not a philosopher now living that can be sure but that there is some other fact to be discovered yet which will upset every hypothesis that he hath sent forth into the world. Philosophers who conceitedly glory over believers in revelation are fools, for they know nothing with certainty, and absolute certainty appertains only to divine revelation. In those who pretend to wisdom apart from God folly abounds. There is no light in them, nor in any man except that which cometh from the Spirit of God. That wisdom which sets itself up apart from God is atheism, because God knoweth, and He saith to man, 'I will teach you, I will reveal myself to you by my Son.' But wisdom says, 'We do not want to be taught: we know of ourselves.' Then you are a rival to God! You pretend to be superior to God, since you are not willing to learn of Him, but will rather trust yourself. This folly and this atheism are the reasons why God hides His mind from the wise and the clever; they reject Him, and therefore He gives them over to a judicial blindness, and Christ thanks Him that He does, for it is but justice that He should do so.

When the Lord is pleased to give to any man a childlike spirit then is he on the road to knowledge. This is true even in science itself. The secrets of nature will never be revealed to the man who believes that he already knows them. Nature herself does not teach the man who comes to her with prejudice. A man who thinks he knows beforehand sits down to study nature, and what does he generally discover? Well, he learnedly dreams of a universal solvent, or that the baser metals can be transmuted into gold, or that there is a perpetual motion. Those, you say, are things philosophers believed years ago. Yes, but their theories of today are just as stupid, and the science of today will be the jest of the next century. The greatest absurdities have been the pets of philosophy for hundreds of years, and why was it that men did not know better? Because they did not go to nature and ask her to teach them what was fact; they made an hypothesis, and then they went to nature to force her to prove it, as they do now; they start with a prejudgment of what they would like to be, and then take facts and twist them round into their system, and so they blind themselves by their own wisdom.

Well, if it be so in nature, and I am sure it is, it is certainly more so in grace, for when a man comes to the word of

God and says, 'Now I know theology beforehand; I do not come here to find my creed in the Bible and learn it like a child, but I come to turn texts about and make them fit into my system.' Well, he will blind himself, and will be a fool, and it is right he should be blinded, for hath he not done that wilfully which must of necessity lead to such an end? Brethren, simple teachableness is the first essential for the reception of a revelation from God, and if you have it today, if you are seeking after truth, if you are crying after her, and if you are willing that God should reveal her to you, if you are anxious that He should reveal truth to you in Christ, you are the sort of person upon whom God in sovereignty looks with divine favour, and unto such as you are will He reveal Himself. What is wanted is faith, a childlike, receptive faith; not faith in a pope, not faith in a man, not faith in an old established creed, but faith in God. Oh, my hearer, be thou willing to learn of Him, and thou shalt not be left uninstructed.

Now a lesson or two, and I have done. The first lesson to be learnt is this. If great men, if eminent men, if so-called learned men, are not converted, do not be cast down about it,-it is not likely they will be. In the next place, if many converts are obscure persons, persons without note or name, do not be at all disgusted with that fact. Who are you that you should be? Who are you that you should despise any upon whom God has looked in favour? Rather rejoice exceedingly with your Lord that God hath chosen the despised, and you with them.

Next, learn that the sovereignty of God is always exercised in such a way that the pure in heart may always rejoice in it. God never did a sovereign act yet that the loving Christ Himself could not rejoice in. Be you content, therefore, to leave everything in the hand of God that you do not understand, and when His way is in the sea, be quite as glad as when His way is in the sanctuary; when His footsteps are not known, feel that they are quite as righteous and quite as holy as when you can perceive the path in which He moves.

The ultimate honour of the gospel is secured unto God alone, let that be our last lesson. When the wind up of all things shall come there shall be no honour to any of us, nor would we desire it; but out of it all, out of the choice of each one, and out of the revelation made to each one, will come up, multiplied into a thousand thunders, the voice as of Christ in His whole mystical body, 'I thank thee, O Father.' This shall be the song of heaven concerning the whole matter, as well concerning the lost as the saved. 'I thank thee, O Father, Lord of heaven and earth.' There shall be no cavils amongst the pure in heart, nor questions among the perfected spirits, but the whole family reviewing the whole of the Father's government, the hiding as well as the revealing, shall at the last say, Christ leading the utterance – 'I thank thee, O Father, Lord of heaven and earth, that thou hast hid these things from the wise and prudent, and hast revealed them unto babes.'

Brothers and sisters, let us learn our need of a personal revelation, let us seek it if we have not yet received it; with a childlike spirit, let us seek it in Christ, for He only can reveal the Father to us; and when we have it let it be our joy that we see Him revealing it to others, and let this be our prayer, that the God of Jacob would yet bring others unto Christ, who shall rejoice in the light that has made glad our eyes. The Lord be with you. Amen.

3

The Joy of the Lord, the Strength of His People

'The joy of the Lord is your strength.'
(Neh. 8:10)

'And the sinners sang aloud, with Jezrahiah their overseer. Also that day they offered great sacrifices, and rejoiced: for God had made them rejoice with great joy: the wives also and the children rejoiced: so that the joy of Jerusalem was heard even afar off.'
(Neh. 12:42, 43)

Last Sabbath day in the morning I spoke of the birth of our Saviour as being full of joy to the people of God, and, indeed, to all nations. We then looked at the joy from a distance; we will now in contemplation draw nearer to it, and perhaps as we consider it, and remark the multiplied reasons for its existence, some of those reasons may operate upon our own hearts, and we may go out of this house of prayer ourselves partakers of the exceeding great joy. We shall count it to have been a successful morning if the people of God are made to rejoice in the Lord, and especially if those who have been bowed down and burdened in soul shall receive the oil of joy for mourning. It is no mean thing to comfort the Lord's mourners; it is a work specially dear to the Spirit of God, and, therefore, not to be lightly esteemed. Holy sorrow is precious before God, and is no bar to godly joy.

Let it be carefully noted in connection with our first text that abounding mourning is no reason why there should not speedily be seen an equally abundant joy; for the very people who were bidden by Nehemiah and Ezra to rejoice were even then melted with penitential grief, 'for all the people wept when they heard the words of the law.' The vast congregation before the Watergate, under the teaching of Ezra, were awakened and cut to the heart; they felt the edge of the law of God like a sword opening up their hearts, tearing, cutting, and killing, and well might they lament; then was the time to let them feel the gospel's balm and hear the gospel's music, and, therefore, the former sons of thunder channelled their note, and became sons of consolation, saying to them, 'This day is holy unto the Lord your God; mourn not, nor weep. Go your way, eat the fat, and drink the sweet, and send portions unto them for whom nothing is prepared: for this day is holy unto our Lord: neither be ye sorry; for the joy of the Lord is your strength.'

Now that they were penitent, and sincerely turned to their God, they were bidden to rejoice. As certain fabrics need to be damped before they will take the glowing colours with which they are to be adorned, so our spirits need the bedecking of repentance before they can receive the radiant colouring of delight. The glad news of the gospel can only be printed on wet paper. Have you ever seen clearer shining than that which follows a shower? Then the sun transforms the raindrops into gems, the flowers look up with fresher smiles and faces glittering from their refreshing bath, and the birds from among the dripping branches sing with notes more rapturous, because they have paused awhile. So, when the soul has been saturated with the rain of penitence, the clear shining of forgiving love makes the flowers of gladness blossom all around. The steps by which we ascend to the palace of delight are usually moist with tears. Grief for sin is the porch of the House Beautiful, where the guests are full of 'the joy of the Lord'. I hope, then, that the mourners, to whom this discourse shall come, will discover and enjoy the meaning of that divine benediction in the Sermon on the Mount, 'Blessed are they that mourn, for they shall be comforted.'

From our text we shall draw several themes of thought, and shall remark: first, *there is a joy of divine origin* – 'The joy of the Lord'; and, secondly, *that joy is to all who partake of it a source of strength* – 'The joy of the Lord is your strength.' Then we shall go on to show that *such strength always reveals itself practically* – our second text will help us there: and we shall close by noticing, in the fourth place, *that this joy, and, consequently, this strength, are within our reach to-day.*

1. There is a Joy of Divine Origin – 'The joy of the Lord.'

Springing from the Lord as its source, it will necessarily be of a very elevated character. Since man fell in the garden, he has too often sought for his enjoyments where the serpent finds his. It is written, 'upon thy belly shalt thou go and dust shalt thou eat all the days of thy life.' This was the serpent's doom; and man, with infatuated ambition, has tried to find his delight in his sensual appetites, and to content his soul with earth's poor dust. But the joys of time cannot satisfy an undying nature, and when a soul is once quickened by the eternal Spirit, it can no more fill itself with worldly mirth, or even with the common enjoyments of life than can a man snuff up wind and feed thereon. But, beloved, we are not left to search for joy; it is brought to our doors by the love of God our Father; joy refined and satisfying, befitting immortal spirits. God has not left us to wander among those unsatisfactory things which mock the chase which they invite; He has given us appetites which carnal things cannot content, and He has provided suitable satisfaction for those appetites; He has stored up at His right hand pleasures for evermore, which even now He reveals by His Spirit to those chosen ones whom He has taught to long for them.

Let us endeavour to analyse that special and peculiar pleasure which is here called 'The joy of the Lord'. *It springs from God, and has God for its object.* The believer who is in a spiritually healthy state rejoices mainly in God Himself; he is happy because there is a God, and because God is in His person and character what He is. All the attributes of God become wellsprings of joy to the thoughtful, contemplative believer; for such a man says within his soul, 'All these attributes of my God are mine: His power, my protection; His wisdom, my guidance; his faithfulness, my foundation; His grace, my salvation.' He is a God who cannot lie, faithful and true to His promise; He is all love, and at the same time infinitely just, supremely holy. Why, the contemplation of God to one who knows that this God is his God for ever and ever, is enough to make the eyes overflow with tears, because of the deep, mysterious, unutterable bliss which fills the heart. There was nothing in the character of Jupiter, or any of the pretended gods of the heathen, to make glad a pure and holy spirit, but there is everything in the character of Jehovah both to purify the heart and to make it thrill with delight. How sweet is it to think over all the Lord has done; how He has revealed Himself of old, and especially how He has displayed His glory in the covenant of grace, and in the person of the Lord Jesus Christ. How charming is the thought that He has revealed Himself to me personally, and made me to see in Him my Father, my friend, my helper, my God. Oh, if there be one word out of heaven that cannot be excelled, even by the brightness of heaven itself, it is this word, 'My God, my Father,' and that sweet promise, 'I will be to them a God, and they shall be to me a people.'

There is no richer consolation to be found: even the Spirit of God can bring nothing home to the heart of the Christian more fraught with delight than that blessed consideration. When the child of God, after admiring the character and wondering at the acts of God, can all the while feel 'he is my God; I have taken Him to be mine; He has taken me to be His; He has grasped me with the hand of his powerful love; having loved me with an everlasting love, with the bands of lovingkindness has He drawn me to Himself; my beloved is mine and I am His,' why, then, his soul would fain dance like David before the ark of the Lord, rejoicing in the Lord with all its might.

A further source of joy is found by the Christian, who is living near to God, in *a deep sense of reconciliation to God, of acceptance with God, and yet, beyond that, of adoption and close relationship to God*. Does it not make a man glad to know that though once his sins had provoked the Lord they are all blotted out, not one of them remaineth; though once he was estranged from God, and far off from Him by wicked works, yet he is made nigh by the blood of Christ. The Lord is no longer an angry judge pursuing us with a drawn sword, but a loving Father into whose bosom we pour our sorrows, and find ease for every pang of heart. Oh, to know, beloved, that God actually loves us! I have often told you I cannot preach upon that theme, for it is a subject to muse upon in silence, a matter to sit by the hour together and meditate upon. The infinite to love an insignificant creature, an ephemera of an hour, a shadow that declineth! Is not this a marvel? For God to pity me I can understand, for God to condescend to have mercy upon me I can comprehend; but for Him to love me, for the pure to love a sinner, for the infinitely great to love a worm, is matchless, a miracle of miracles! Such thoughts must comfort the soul. And then, add to this, that the divine love has brought as believers into actual relationship with God, so that we are His sons and daughters, this again is a river of sacred pleasure. 'Unto which of the angels said he at any time, Thou art my Son?' No minister of flame, though perfect in obedience, has received the honour of adoption; to us, even to us frail creatures of the dust, is given a boon denied to Gabriel, for through Jesus Christ the firstborn, we are members of the family of God. Oh! the abyss of joy which lies in sonship with God, and joint heirship with Christ! Words are vain here.

Moreover, the joy springing from the spirit of adoption is another portion of the believer's bliss. He cannot be an unhappy man who can cry, 'Abba, Father.' The spirit of adoption is always attended by love, joy, and peace, which are fruits of the Spirit; for we have not received the spirit of bondage again to fear, but we have received the spirit of liberty and joy in Christ Jesus. 'My God, my Father.' Oh how sweet the sound. But all men of God do not enjoy this, say you. Alas! we grant it, but we also add that it is their own fault. It is the right and portion of every believer to live in the assurance that he is reconciled to God, that God loves him, and that he is God's child, and if he doth not so live he has himself only to blame. If there be any starving at God's table, it is because the guest stints himself, for the feast is superabundant. If however, a man comes, and I pray you all may, to live habitually under a sense of pardon through the sprinkling of the precious blood, and in a delightful sense of perfect reconciliation with the great God, he is the possessor of a joy unspeakable and full of glory.

But, beloved, this is not all. The joy of the Lord in the spirit springs also from *an assurance that all the future, whatever it may be, is guaranteed by divine goodness,* that being children of God, the love of God towards us is not of a mutable character, but abides and remains unchangeable. The believer feels an entire satisfaction in leaving himself in the hands of eternal and immutable love. However happy I may be today, if I am in doubt concerning tomorrow, there is a worm at the root of my peace; although the past may now be sweet in retrospect, and the present fair in enjoyment, yet if the future be grim with fear, my joy is but shallow. If my salvation be still a matter of hazard and jeopardy, unmingled joy is not mine, and deep peace is still out of my reach. But when I know that He whom I have rested in hath power and grace enough to complete that which He hath begun in me, and for me; when I see the work of Christ to be no half-way redemption, but a complete and eternal salvation; when I perceive that the promises are established upon an unchangeable basis, and are yea and amen in Christ Jesus, ratified by oath and sealed by blood, then my soul hath perfect contentment.

It is true that looking forward there may be seen long avenues of tribulation, but the glory is at the end of them; battles may be foreseen, and woe unto the man who does not expect them, but the eye of faith perceives the crown of victory. Deep waters are mapped upon our journey, but faith can see Jehovah fording these rivers with us, and she anticipates the day when we shall ascend the banks of the hither shore and enter into Jehovah's rest. When we have received these priceless truths into our souls we are satisfied with favour and full of the goodness of the Lord. There is a theology which denies to believers this consolation; we will not enter into controversy with it, but sorrowfully hint that a heavy chastisement for the errors of that system of doctrine lies in the loss of the comfort which the truth would have brought into the soul. For my part, I value the gospel not only for what it has done for me in the past, but for the guarantees which it affords me of eternal salvation. 'I give unto my sheep eternal life, and they shall never perish, neither shall any pluck them out of my hand.'

Now, beloved, I have not yet taken you into the great deeps of joy, though these streams are certainly by no means shallow. There is an abyss of delight for every Christian *when he comes into actual fellowship with God.* I spoke of the truth that God loved us, and the fact that we are related to Him by ties most near and dear; but, oh, when these doctrines become experiences, then are we indeed anointed with the oil of gladness. When we enter into the love of God, and it enters into us; when we walk with God habitually, then our joy is like Jordan at harvest time, when it overfloweth all its banks. Do you know what it means to walk with God – Enoch's joy; to sit at Jesus' feet – Mary's joy; to lean your head upon Jesus' bosom – John's familiar joy? Oh yes, communion with the Lord is no mere talk with some of us. We have known it in the chamber of affliction; we have known it in the solitude of many a night of broken rest; we have known it beneath discouragements and under sorrows and defamations, and all sorts of ills; and we reckon that one dram of fellowship with Christ is enough to sweeten an ocean full of tribulation, and that only to know that He is near us, and to see the gleaming of His dear eye, would transform even hell itself into heaven, if it were possible for us to enjoy His presence there. Alas! ye do not and cannot know this bliss, ye who quaff your foaming bowls, listening to the sound of stringed instruments, ye do not know what this bliss means – ye have not dreamed of it, nor could ye compass it though a man should tell it unto you. As the beast in the meadow knows not the far-reaching thoughts of him who reads the stars and threads the spheres, so neither can the carnal man make so much as a guess of what are the joys which God hath prepared for them that love Him, which any day and every day, when our hearts seek it, He revealeth unto us by His Spirit. This is 'the joy of the Lord', fellowship with the Father and with His Son Jesus Christ. Beloved, if we reach this point, we must labour to maintain our standing, for our Lord saith to us, 'abide in me.' The habit of communion is the life of happiness.

Another form of 'the joy of the Lord' will visit us practically every day in the *honour of being allowed* to *serve Him*. It is a joy worth worlds to be allowed to do good. To teach a little child his letters for Christ, will give a true heart some taste of the joy of the Lord, if it be consciously done for the Lord's sake alone. To bear the portion to those for whom nothing is prepared, to visit the sick, to comfort the mourner, to aid the poor, to instruct the ignorant, any, and all of such Christian works, if done in Jesus' name, will in their measure array us in Jehovah's joy. And happy are we, brethren, if when we cannot work we are enabled to lie still and suffer, for acquiescence is another silver pipe through which 'the joy of the Lord' will come to us. It is sweet to smart beneath God's rod, and feel that if God would have us suffer it is happiness to do so, to fall back with the faintness of nature, but at the same time with the strength of grace, and say, 'Thy will be done.' It is joy, when between millstones crushed like an olive, to yield nothing but the oil of thankfulness; when bruised beneath the flail of tribulation, still to lose nothing but the chaff; and to yield to God the precious grain of entire submissiveness. Why, this is a little heaven upon earth. To glory in tribulations also, this is a high degree of upclimbing towards the likeness of our Lord. Perhaps, the usual communions which we have with our Beloved, though exceeding precious, will never equal those which we enjoy when we have to break through thorns and briars to be at Him; when we follow Him into the wilderness then we feel the love of our espousals to be doubly sweet. It is a joyous thing when in the midst of mournful circumstances, we yet feel that we cannot mourn because the Bridegroom is with us. Blessed is that man who, in the most terrible storm, is driven not from his God, but even rides upon the crest of the lofty billows nearer towards heaven. Such happiness is the Christian's lot. I do not say that every

Christian possesses it, but I am sure that every Christian ought to do so. There is a highway to heaven, and all in it are safe; but in the middle of that road there is a special way, an inner path, and all who walk therein are happy as well as safe. Many professors are only just within the hedge, they walk in the ditch by the road side, and because they are safe there, they are content to put up with all the inconveniences of their walk; but he who takes the crown of the causeway, and walks in the very centre of the road that God has cast up, shall find that no lion shall be there, neither shall any ravenous beast go up thereon, for there the Lord Himself shall be his companion, and will manifest Himself to him. You shallow Christians who do but believe in Christ, and barely that, whose Bibles are unread, whose closets are unfrequented, whose communion with God is a thing of spasms, you have not the joy of the Lord, neither are you strong. I beseech you, rest not as you are, but let your conscious feebleness provoke you to seek the means of strength: and that means of strength is to be found in a pleasant medicine, sweet as it is profitable – the delicious and effectual medicine of 'the joy of the Lord'.

2. But time would fail me to prolong our remarks upon this very fruitful subject, and we shall turn to our second head, which is **that this joy is a source of great strength**.

Very rapidly let us consider this thought. It is so because this joy arises from considerations which always strengthen the soul. Very much of the depth of our piety will depend upon our thoughtfulness. Many persons, after having received a doctrine, put it by on the shelf; they are orthodox, they have received the truth, and they are content to keep that truth on hand as dead stock. Sirs, of what account can this be to you, to store your garners with wheat if you never grind the corn for bread, or sow it in the furrows of your fields? He is the joyful Christian who uses the doctrines of the gospel for spiritual meat, as they were meant to be used. Why, some men might as well have a heterodox creed as an orthodox one for all the difference it makes to them. Having the notion that they know, and imagining that to know sufficeth them, they do not consider, contemplate, or regard the truths which they profess to believe, and, consequently, they derive no benefit from them. Now, to contemplate the great truths of divine election, of eternal love, of covenant engagements, of justification by faith through the blood of Christ, and the indwelling and perpetual abiding of the Holy Ghost in His people – to turn over these things is to extract joy from them; and this also is strengthening to the mind. To press the heavenly grapes by meditation, and make the red wine flow forth in torrents, is an exercise as strengthening as it is exhilarating. Joy comes from the same truths which support our strength, and comes by the process of meditation.

Again, 'the joy of the Lord' within us is always the sign and symbol of strong spiritual life. Holy vivacity betokens spiritual vigour. I said that he who had spiritual joy gained it by communion with God, but communion with God is the surest fosterer of strength. You cannot be with a strong God without getting strength yourself, for God is always a transforming God; regarding and looking upon Him our likeness changes till we become in our measure like our God. The warmth of the south of France, of which you often hear so much, does not spring from soft balmy winds, but from the sun; at sunset the temperature falls. You shall be on one side of the street in Italy and think it May, cross the street into the shade and it is cold as January. The sun does it all. A man who walks in the sunlight of God's countenance, for that very reason is warm and strong. The sunlight of joy usually goes with the warmth of spiritual life. As the light of joy varies so does the warmth of holy strength; he who dwells in the light of God is both happy and strong. He who goes into the shade and loses the joy of the Lord becomes weak at the same time. So the joy of the Lord becomes our strength, as being an indicator of its rise or fall. When a soul is really vigorous and active, it is like the torrent which dashes down the mountainside, which scorns in winter to own the bonds of frost: in a few hours the stagnant pools and slowly moving streams are enchained in ice; but the snow king must bring forth all his strength ere he can manacle the rushing torrent. So when a soul dashes on with the sacred force of faith, it is hard to freeze it into misery, its vigour secures its joy.

Furthermore, the man who possesses 'the joy of the Lord' finds it his strength in another respect, that it fortifies him against temptation. What is there that he can be tempted with? He has more already than the world can offer him as a reward for treachery. He is already rich; who shall ensnare him with the wages of unrighteousness? He is already satisfied; who is he that can seduce him with pleasing baits? 'Shall such a man as I flee?' The rejoicing Christian is equally proof against persecution. They may well afford to be laughed at who win at such a rate as he does. 'You may scoff,' saith he, 'but I know what true religion is within my soul, and your scoffing will not make me relinquish the pearl of great price.' Such a man is, moreover, made strong to bear affliction; for all the sufferings put upon him are but a few drops of bitterness cast into his cup of bliss, to give a deeper tone to the sweetness which absorbs them.

Such a man becomes strong for service, too. What can he not do who is happy in his God? By his God he leaps over a wall, or breaks through a troop. Strong is he, too, for any kind of self-sacrifice. To the God who gives him all, and remains to him as his perpetual portion, such a man gives up all that he hath, and thinks it no surrender. It is but laying up his treasure in his own peculiar treasure house, even in the God of his salvation.

A joyous man, such I have now in my mind's eye, is to all intents and purposes a strong man. He is strong in a calm restful manner. Whatever happens he is not ruffled or disturbed. He is not afraid of evil tidings, his heart is fixed, trusting in the Lord. The ruffled man is ever weak. He is in a hurry, and doth things ill. The man full of joy within is quiet, he bides his time and croucheth in the fullness of his strength. Such a man, though he is humble, is firm and steadfast; he is not carried away with every wind, or bowed by every breeze, he knows what he knows, and holds what he holds, and the golden anchor of his hope entereth within the veil, and holds him fast. His strength is not pretentious but real. The happiness arising from communion with God breeds in him no boastfulness; he does not talk of what he can do, but he does it; he does not say what he could bear, but he bears all that comes. He does not himself always know what he could do; his weakness is the more apparent to himself because of the strength which the Holy Ghost puts upon him; but when the time comes, his weakness only illustrates the divine might, while the man goes calmly on, conquering and to conquer. His inner light makes him independent of the outward sun; his secret granaries make him independent of the outer harvest; his inward fountains place him beyond dread though the brook Cherith may dry up; he is independent of men and angels, and fearless of devils; all creatures may turn against him if they please, but since God Himself is his exceeding joy, he will not miss their love or mourn their hate. He standeth where others fall, he sings where others weep, he wins where others fly, he glorifies his God where others bring dishonour on themselves and on the sacred name. God grant us the inward joy which arises from real strength and is so linked with it as to be in part its cause.

3. But now I must hasten on to notice in the third place **that this strength leads to practical results**. I am sure I shall have your earnest attention to this, because in many of you I have seen the results follow of which I now speak. I would not flatter anyone, but my heart has been full of thanksgiving to the God of all grace when I have seen many of you rejoicing in the Lord under painful circumstances and producing the fruits of a gracious strength. Turn then to our second text, and there you shall observe some of the fruits of holy joy and pious strength.

First, it leads to *great praise*. 'The singers sang aloud,' their minstrelsy was hearty and enthusiastic. Sacred song is not a minor matter. Quaint George Herbert has said, 'Praying's the end of preaching.' Might he not have gone further and have said, *praising's the end of praying*? After all, preaching and praying are not the chief end of man, but the glorifying of God, of which praising God vocally is one form. Preaching is sowing, prayer is watering, but praise is the harvest. God aims at His own glory so should we; and 'whoso offereth praise glorifieth me, saith the Lord.' Be ye diligent then to sing His praises with understanding. We have put away harps and trumpets and organs, let us mind that we really rise above the need of them. I think we do well to dispense with these helps of the typical dispensation; they are all inferior even in music to the human voice, there is assuredly no melody or harmony like those created by living tongues; but let us mind that we do not put away an atom of the joy. Let us be glad when in the congregation we unite in psalmody.

It is a wretched thing to hear the praises of God rendered professionally, as if the mere music were everything. It is horrible to have a dozen people in the table-pew singing for you, as if they were proxies for the whole assembly. It is shocking to me to be present in places of worship where not a tenth of the people ever venture to sing at all, and these do it through their teeth so very softly, that one had need to have a microscope invented for his ears, to enable him to hear the dying strain. Out upon such mumbling and murdering of the praises of God; if men's hearts were joyous and strong, they would scorn such miserable worship. In this house we all try to sing, but might we not have more praise services? We have had a praise meeting every now and then. Ought we not to hold a praise meeting every week? Should not the prayer meeting be more than ever cheered by praise? The singing of God's people should be, and if they were more full of divine strength would be, more constant and universal. How sinners chant the praise of Bacchus in the streets! You can hardly rest in the middle of the night, but what unseemly sounds of revelry startle you. Shall the votaries of wine sing so lustily, and shall we be silent? We are not often guilty of disturbing the world with our music; the days in which Christian zeal interfered with the wicked seem to have gone by; we have settled down into more orderliness, and I am afraid also into more lukewarmness. Oh for the old Methodistic shout. Brethren, wake up your singing again. May the Lord give us again a singing-time, and make us all praise Him with heart, and with voice, till even the adversaries shall say, 'The Lord hath done great things for them'; and we shall reply, 'Ay, ye speak the truth; he hath done great things for us, whereof we are glad.'

Perhaps there has not been so large a blessing upon the churches of England, because they have not rendered due thanksgiving. In all the time in which we are in trouble we are anxious and prayerful; when a prince is sick bulletins are issued every hour or so, but ah, when the mercy comes but few bulletins are put out, calling upon us to bless and praise the name of God for His mercies. Let us praise the Lord from the rising of the sun unto the going down of the same, for great is the Lord, and greatly is He to be praised.

The next result is *great sacrifice*. 'That day they offered great sacrifices and rejoiced.' What day is that in which the church of God now makes great sacrifices? I have not seen it in the calendar of late. And, alas! if men make any sacrifice they very often do so in a mode which indicates that they would escape the inflection if they could. Few make great sacrifices and rejoice. You can persuade a man to give a considerable sum; a great many arguments at last overcome him, and he does it because he would have been ashamed not to do it, but in his heart he wishes you had not come that way, and had gone to some other donor. That is the most acceptable gift to God which is given rejoicingly. It is well to feel that whatever good your gift may do to the church or the poor or the sick, it is twice as much benefit to you to give it. It is well to give, because you love to give; as the flower which pours forth its perfume because it never dreamed of doing otherwise; or like the bird which quivers with song, because it is a bird and finds a pleasure in its notes; or like the sun which shines, not by constraint, but because, being a sun, it must shine; or like the waves of the sea which flash back the brilliance of the sun, because it is their nature to reflect and not to hoard the light. Oh, to have such grace in our hearts that we shall joyfully make sacrifices unto our God. The Lord grant that we may have much of this; for the bringing of the tithes into the storehouse is the way to the blessing; as saith the Scripture: 'Bring ye all the tithes into the storehouse, that there may be meat in thine house, and prove me now herewith, saith the Lord of hosts, if I will not open you the windows of heaven, and pour you out a blessing, that there shall not be room enough to receive it.'

Next to that, there are sure to follow *other expressions of joy*. They 'rejoiced, for God had made them to rejoice with great joy.' It was not all singing and giving. When the wheels of the machine are well oiled the whole machine goes easily; and when the man has the oil of joy, then in his business, and in his family, the wheels of his nature glide along sweetly and harmoniously, because he is a glad and a happy man. There are some professors who imagine the sorrow of the Lord to be their strength; they glory in the spirit of bondage and in an unbelieving experience, having great acquaintance with the corruption of their hearts, sometimes of a rather too practical character. They make the deformities of the saints to be their beauty-spots, and their faults to be their evidences. Such men denounce all who rejoice in the Lord, and only tolerate the unbelieving. Their strength lies in being able to take you through all the catacombs of nature's darkness, and to show you the rottenness of their evil hearts. Well, such strength as that let those have who will, but we are persuaded that our text is nearer to wisdom: 'The joy of the Lord is your strength.' While we know something of our corruption, and mourn it, know something of the world's troubles, and sometimes lament as we bear them; yet there is a joy in the perfect work of Christ, and a joy in our union to Him which uplifts us far above all other considerations. God becomes to us such a strength that we cannot help showing our joy in our ordinary life.

But then the text tells us that holy joy leads to *family happiness*. 'The wives also and the children rejoiced.' It is so in this church. I have lately seen several children from households which God has blessed, and I have rejoiced to see that father and mother know the Lord, and that even the last of the family has been brought to Jesus. O happy households where the joy is not confined to one, but where all partake of it. I dislike much that Christianity which makes a man feel, 'If I go to heaven it is all I care for.' Why, you are like a German stove which I found in the room of an hotel the other day – a kind of stove which required all the wood they could bring up merely to warm itself, and then all the heat went up the chimney. We sat around it to make it warm, but scarce a particle of heat came forth from it to us. Too many need all the religion they can get to cheer their own hearts, and their poor families and neighbours sit shivering in the cold of ungodliness. Be like those well-constructed stoves of our own houses, which send out all the heat into the room. Send out the heat of piety into your house, and let all the neighbours participate in the blessing, for so the text finishes, 'The joy of Jerusalem was heard afar off.' The joy of the Lord should be observed throughout our neighbourhood, and many who might otherwise have been careless of true religion will then enquire, 'What makes these people glad, and creates such happy households?' Your joy shall thus be God's missionary.

4. And now I have to close. **This Joy, This Strength, are Both Within our Reach.** 'For the Lord had made them glad with great joy.' God alone can give us this great joy. Then it is within the reach of any, for God can give it to one as well as to another. If it depended upon our good works or our natural abilities, some of us could never reach it; but if God is the source and giver of it He may give it to me as well as to thee, my brother, and to thee as well as to another. What was the way in which God gave this joy? Well first, He gave it to these people by their being *attentive hearers*. They were not only hearers, but they heard with their ears, their ears were into the word; it was read to them and they sucked it in, receiving it into their souls. An attentive hearer is on the way to being a joyous receiver. Having heard it they *felt the power of it*, and they wept.

Did that seem the way to joy? It was. They received the threatenings of the law with all their terrors into their soul, they allowed the hammer of the word to break them in pieces, they submitted themselves to the word of reproof. Oh! that God would incline you all to do the same, for this, again, is the way in which God gives joy. The word is heard, the word is felt. Then after this, when they had felt the power of the word, we see that *they worshipped God devoutly*. They bowed the head. Their postures indicated what they felt within. Worshippers who with penitent hearts really adore God, will never complain of weary Sabbaths; adoration helps us into joy. He who can bow low enough before the throne shall be lifted as high before that throne as his heart can desire.

We read also that these hearers and worshippers *understood* clearly what they heard. Never be content with hearing a sermon unless you can understand it, and if there be a truth that is above you, strain after it, strive to know it. Bible-reader, do not be content with going through the words of the chapter: pray the Holy Ghost to tell you the meaning, and use proper means for finding out that meaning; ask those who know, and use your own enlightened judgment to discover the sense. When shall we have done with formalism of worship and come into living adoration? Sometimes, for all the true singing that there is, the song might as well be in Latin or in Greek. Oh! to know what you are singing, to know what you are saying in prayer, to know what you are reading, to get at it, to come right into it, to understand it — this is the way to holy joy.

And one other point. These people when they had understood what they had devoutly heard, were *eager to obey*. They obeyed not only the common points of the law in which Israel of old had furnished them with examples, but they found out an old institution which had been buried and forgotten. What was that to them? God had commanded it, and they celebrated it, and in so doing this peculiar joy came upon them. Oh, for the time when all believers shall search the word of God, when they shall not be content with saying, 'I have joined myself with a certain body of Christians, and they do so; therefore I do so.' May no man say to himself any longer, 'Such is the rule of my church,' but may each say, 'I am God's servant and not the servant of man, not the servant of Thirty-Nine Articles, of the Prayer-book, or the Catechism; I stand to my own Master, and the only law book I acknowledge is the book of His word, inspired by His Spirit.' Oh, blessed day, when every man shall say, 'I want to know wherein I am wrong; I desire to know what I am to do; I am anxious to follow the Lord fully.' Well, then, if your joy in God leads you to practical obedience, you may rest assured it has made you strong in the very best manner.

Beloved brethren and sisters, we had, before I went away for needed rest, a true spirit of prayer among us. I set out for the Continent joyfully, because I left with you the names of some eighty persons proposed for church membership. My beloved officers, with great diligence, have visited these and others, and next Lord's Day we hope to receive more than a hundred, perhaps a hundred and twenty, fresh members into the church. Blessed be God for this. I should not have felt easy in going away if you had been in a barren, cold, dead state; but there was a real fire blazing on God's altar, and souls were being saved. Now, I desire that this gracious zeal should continue, and be renewed. It has not gone out in my absence, I believe, but I desire now a fresh blast from God's Spirit to blow the flame very vehemently. Let us meet for prayer tomorrow, and let the prayer be very earnest, and let those wrestlers who have been moved to agonising supplication renew the ardour and fervency of their desires, and may we be a strong people, and consequently a joyous people in the strength and joy of the Lord. May sinners in great numbers look unto Jesus and be saved!

4

Joy, Joy For Ever

'But let all those that put their trust in thee rejoice: let them ever shout for joy, because thou defendest them: let them also that love thy name be joyful in thee'.
(Ps. 5:11)

'The Lord doth put a difference between the Egyptians and Israel.' There is an ancient difference which He has made in His eternal purpose; and this is seen in every item of the covenant of grace. 'The Lord hath set apart him that is godly for himself.' But it is also written, 'The foolish shall not stand in thy sight: thou hatest all workers of iniquity.' You that have believed are of the house of Israel, and heirs according to promise; for they that are of faith are the true seed of faithful Abraham. See that ye make manifest this difference by the holiness of your lives. 'Come out from among them, and be ye separate, saith the Lord, and touch not the unclean thing.' Evermore display this difference by the joyfulness of your spirits. Let not noisome cares invade you; for we read, 'I will sever in that day the land of Goshen, in which my people dwell, that no swarms of flies shall be there.' Fear not that the wrathful judgment of God will fall indiscriminately; for we read, 'Only in the land of Goshen, where the children of Israel were, was there no hail.' The servants of the Lord should wear the royal livery: that livery is made of the fine cloth of holiness, trimmed with the lace of joy. Take care that you exhibit both holiness of character and joyfulness of spirit; for where these two things are in us, and abound, they make us that we be not barren nor unfruitful. To us there should be joy, strikingly to contrast with the unrest of the unbeliever. Over all the land of Egypt there was darkness which might be felt, even thick darkness, for three days: 'They saw not one another, neither rose any from his place for three days: but all the children of Israel had light in their dwellings.' If it be so with you, that the Lord has given you the light of joy, let your faces shine with it. If you walk in the light as God is in the light, go forth and let men see the brightness of your countenances, and take knowledge of you that you have been with Jesus, and have learned of Him His gracious calm, as well as His holiness. 'Rejoice in the Lord alway.' Your Lord desires that your joy may be full. He gives you a joy which no man taketh from you: it is His legacy. 'Peace I leave with you, my peace I give unto you: not as the world giveth, give I unto you.'

The subject for this morning is joy, the joy of faith, the joy which is the fruit of the Spirit from the root of trust in God. May we not only talk about it at this hour, but enjoy it now and evermore! It is pleasant to read, and hear, and think about joy; but to be filled with joy and peace through believing is a far more satisfying thing. I want you to see not only the sparkling fountain of joy, but to drink deep draughts of it; yes, and drink all the week, and all the month, and all the year, and all the rest of your lives, both in time and in eternity. 'Let the children of Zion be joyful in their King.'

First, let us speak a little upon **the kind of joy which is allotted to believers**: 'Let all those that put their trust in thee rejoice: let them ever shout for joy, because thou defendest them: let them also that love thy name be joyful in thee.'

Note, first, concerning this joy, that *it is to be universal to all who trust*: 'Let all those that put their trust in thee rejoice.' This is not only for the healthy, but for the sickly; not only for the successful, but for the disappointed; not only for those who have the bird in the hand, but for those who only see it in the bush. Let all rejoice! If you have but a little faith, yet if you are trusting in the Lord, you have a right to joy. It may be, your joy will not rise so high as it might do if your faith were greater; but still, where faith is true, it gives sure ground for joy. O ye babes in grace, ye little children, you that have been newly converted, and sadly feel your feebleness, yet rejoice; for the Lord will bless them that fear Him, 'both small and great!' 'Fear not, thou worm Jacob.' 'Fear not, little flock.' There is a joy which is as milk to nourish babes – a joy which is not as meat with bones in it; for the Lord addeth no sorrow therewith. The little ones of the flock need not vex themselves concerning the deep things of God; for there is joy in those shallows of simple truth where lambs may safely wade. The joy of the Lord is softened down to feeble constitutions, lest it overpower them. The same great sea which floods the vast bays also flows into the tiny creeks. 'Let all those that put their trust in thee rejoice.' You, Miss Much-afraid, over yonder, you are to rejoice! You, Mr Despondency, hardly daring to look up, you must yet learn to sing. As for Mr Ready-to-halt, he must dance on his crutches, and Feeble-mind must play the music for him. It is the mind of the Holy Ghost that those who trust in the Lord should rejoice before Him.

This joy, in the next place, is to be *as constant as to time as it is universal as to persons*. 'Let them ever shout for joy.' Do not be content that a good time in the morning should be followed by dreariness in the afternoon. Do not cultivate an occasional delight, but aim at perpetual joy. To be happy at a revival meeting, and then go home to groan, is a poor business. We should 'feel like singing all the time'. The believer has abiding arguments for abiding consolation. There is never a time when the saint of God has not great cause for gladness; and if he never doubts and worries till he has a justifiable reason for distrust, he will never doubt nor worry. 'Rejoice in the Lord alway, and again' – what? 'alway', and yet does the apostle say, 'and again'? Yes, he would have us rejoice, and keep on rejoicing, and then rejoice more and more. Brethren go on piling up your delights. You are the blessed of the Lord, and His blessing reaches 'unto the utmost bound of the everlasting hills'.

Next, *let your joy be manifested*. 'Let them ever shout for joy.' Shouting is an enthusiastic utterance, a method which men use when they have won a victory, when they divide the spoil, when they bear home the harvest, when they tread the vintage, when they drain the goblet. Believers, you may shout for joy with unreserved delight. Some religionists shout, and we would not wish to stop them; but we wish certain of them knew better what they are shouting for. Brethren, since you know whom you have believed, and what you have believed, and what are the deep sources of your joy, do not be so sobered by your knowledge as to become dumb; but the rather imitate the children in the temple, who, if they knew little, loved much, and so shouted in praise of Him they loved. 'Let them shout for joy.'

A touch of enthusiasm would be the salvation of many a man's religion. Some Christians are good enough people: they are like wax candles, but they are not lighted. Oh, for a touch of flame! Then would they scatter light, and thus become of service to their families. 'Let them shout for joy.' Why not? Let not orderly folks object. One said to me the other day, 'When I hear you preach I feel as if I must have a shout!' My friend, shout if you feel forced to do so. [Here a hearer cried, 'Glory!'] Our brother cries, 'Glory!' and I say so too, 'Glory!' The shouting need not always be done in a public service, or it might hinder devout hearing; but there are times and places where a glorious outburst of enthusiastic joy would quicken life in all around. The ungodly are not half so restrained in their blasphemy as we are in our praise. How is this? They go home making night hideous with their yells: are we never to have an outbreak of consecrated delight? Yes, we will have our high days and holidays, and we will sing and shout for joy till even the heathen say, 'The Lord hath done great things for them.'

This joy *is to be repeated with variations*. One likes, in music, to hear the same tune played in different ways. So here you have it. 'Let them rejoice. Let them ever shout for joy. Let them be joyful in thee.' There is no monotony in real joy. In the presence of mirth one grows dull; but in living joy there is exhilaration. Commend me to the springing well of heavenly joy: its waters are always fresh, clear, sparkling, springing up unto everlasting life. Joy blends many colours in its one ray of light. At times it is quiet, and sits still beneath a weight of glory. I have known it weep, not salt drops, but sweet showers. Have you never cried because of your joy in the Lord? Sometimes joy labours for expression till it is ready to faint; and anon it sings till it rivals the angels. Singing is the natural language of joy; but oftentimes silence suits it even better. Our joy abides in Christ, whether we are quiet or shouting, whether we fall at our Lord's feet as dead, or lean on His bosom in calm delight.

This joy is logical. When I was a child, and went to school, I remember learning out of a book called *Why and Because*. Things one learns as a child stick in the memory; and therefore I like a text which has a 'because' in it. Here it is: 'Let them ever shout for joy, because thou defendest them.' Emotions are not fired by logic; and yet reasons furnish fuel for the flame. A man may be sad, though he cannot explain his sadness, or he may be greatly glad, though he cannot set forth the reasons for his joy. The joy of a believer in God has a firm foundation: it is not the baseless fabric of a vision. The joy of faith burns like coals of juniper, and yet it can be calmly explained and justified. The joyful believer is no lunatic, carried away by a delusion: he has a 'because' with which to account for all his joy – a reason which he can consider on his bed in the night-watches, or defend against a scoffing world. We have a satisfactory reason for our most exuberant joy: 'The Lord hath done great things for us; whereof we are glad.' Philosophers can be happy without music, and saints can be happy despite circumstances. With joy we draw water out of deeper and fuller wells than such as father Jacob digged. Our mirth is as soberly reasonable as the worldling's fears.

Once more, the happiness is *a thing of the heart*; for the text runs thus – 'Let them that *love thy name* be joyful in thee.' We love God. I trust I am speaking to many who could say, 'Lord, thou knowest all things; thou knowest that I love thee.' Is it not a very happy emotion? What is sweeter than to say, with the tears in one's eyes, 'My God, I love thee!' To sit down and have nothing to ask for, no words to utter, but only for the soul to love, is not this heavenly? Measureless depths of unutterable love are in the soul, and in those depths we find the pearl of joy. When the heart is taken up with so delightful an object as the ever-blessed God, it feels an intensity of joy which cannot be rivalled. When our whole being is steeped in adoring love, then heaven comes streaming down, and we rejoice with joy unspeakable and full of glory. I feel I am talking in a poor way about the richest things which are enjoyed by saintly men. Many of you know as much about these matters as I do, perhaps more. But my soul doth even now magnify the Lord, and my spirit doth rejoice in God my Saviour. Although I feel unworthy and unfit to speak to this vast throng, yet I have a great sympathy with my text, for I am 'glad in the Lord'.

Oh, what immortal joys I feel,
And raptures all divine
For Jesus tells me I am his,
And my Beloved mine!

If you sit before the Lord at this time, and indulge your souls with an outflow of love to God and His Son Jesus Christ, and at the same time perceive an inflowing of heavenly joy, it will not much matter how the poor preacher speaks to your ear, for the Lord Himself will be heard in your soul, and heaven will flood your being.

Now I come to the second head, wherein we will consider **the ground and reason of holy joy**. I am bound to speak upon this matter; for I have told you that the joy of the believer is logical, and can be defended by facts; and so indeed it is.

For, first, *the believer's joy arises from the God in whom he trusts.* 'Let all those that put their trust in *thee* rejoice.' When, after many a weary wandering, the dove of your soul has at last come back to the ark, and Noah has put out his hand and 'pulled her in unto him', the poor, weary creature is happy. Taken into Noah's hand and made to nestle in his bosom, she feels so safe, so peaceful! The weary leagues of the wild waste of waters are all forgotten, or only remembered to give zest to the repose. So, when you trust in God, your soul has found a quiet resting-place, a pavilion of repose! The little chick runs to and fro in fear. The mother hen calls it home. She spreads her soft wings over the brood. Have you never seen the little chicks when they are housed under the hen, how they put out their little heads through the feathers and peep and twitter so prettily? It is a chick's heaven to hide under its mother's bosom. It is perfectly happy; it could not be more content; its little chick nature is brim-full of delight. Be this thy joy also, 'He shall cover thee with his feathers, and under his wings shalt thou trust: his truth shall be thy shield and buckler.' My nature gets all its wants supplied, all its desires gratified, when it rests in God. Oh, you that have never trusted God in Christ Jesus, you do not know what real happiness means! You may search all the theatres in London, and ransack all the music-halls, and clubs, and public houses, but you will find no happiness in any of their mirth, or show, or wine. True joy dwells where dwells the living God, and nowhere else. In your own home with God, even though that home be only a single room, and your meal be very scanty, you will see more of heaven than in the palaces of kings! Have God for your sole trust, and you shall never lack for joy.

Our joy arises next *from what the Lord does for us.* 'Let them shout for joy, because *thou defended them.*' God always guards His people, whoever may attack them. 'The Lord is thy keeper.' Angels are our guardians, providence is our protector; but God Himself is the preserver of His chosen. 'Thou shalt not be afraid for the terror by night; nor for the arrow that flieth by day; nor for the pestilence that walketh in darkness; nor for the destruction that wasteth at noonday.' No fortress guards the soldier so well as God guards His redeemed. The God of our salvation will defend us from all evil, He will defend our souls. 'Though an host should encamp against me, my heart shall not fear: though war should rise against me, in this will I be confident.'

Further, *our joy arises out of the love we have towards our God.* 'Let them that love thy name be joyful in thee.' The more you love God, the more you will delight in Him. It is the profusion of a mother's love to her child which makes her take such delight in it. Her boy is her joy because of her love. If we loved Jesus better, we should be happier in Him. You do not, perhaps, see the connection between the two things; but there is a connection so intimate, that little love *to* Christ brings little joy *in* Christ, and great love *to* Christ brings great joy *in* Christ. God grant that in a full Christ we may have a full joy! Do you see what I mean? When a man comes to God in Christ and says, 'This Saviour is my Saviour, this Father is my Father, this God is my God for ever and ever,' then he has everything, and he must be joyful. He has no fear about the past – God has forgiven him; he has no distress about the present – the Lord is with him; he is not afraid about the future – for the Lord hath said, 'I will never leave thee, nor forsake thee.' If you understand my text, and put it in practice, you possess the quintessence of happiness, the essential oil of joy. He that hath joy in his barn floor may see it bare; he that hath joy in his wine vats may see them dry; he that hath joy in his children may bury that joy in the grave; he that hath joy in himself will find his beauty consume away; but he that hath joy in God drinketh from 'the deep which lieth under'; his springs shall ever flow, 'in summer and in winter shall it be.'

I have pointed to the deep sources from which the joy of the believer wells up; but I must also add, it is by faith that this joy comes to us. *Faith makes joyful discoveries.* I speak to those of you who have faith. When you first believed in Christ you found that you were saved, and knew that you were forgiven. Some little while after, you discovered that you were chosen of God from before the foundation of the world. Oh, the rapture of your soul, when the Lord appeared of old unto you, saying, 'Yea, I have loved thee with an everlasting love: therefore with lovingkindness have I drawn thee!' The glorious doctrine of election is as wines on the lees well refined to those who by faith receive it; and it brings with it a new, intense, and refined joy, such as the world knows nothing of. Having discovered your election of God, you looked further into your justification; 'for whom he called, them he also justified.' What a pearl is justification! In Christ the believer is as just in the sight of God as if he had never sinned: he is covered with a perfect righteousness, and is accepted in the Beloved. What a joy is justification by faith, when it is well understood! What bliss also to learn our union to Christ! Believers are members of His body, of His flesh, and of His bones. Because He lives, we shall live also. One with Jesus! Wonderful discovery this! Equally full of joy is our adoption! 'Beloved, now are we the sons of God'; 'And if children, then heirs; heirs of God, and joint-heirs with Christ.' Faith thus heaps fuel on the fire of our joy; for it keeps on making discoveries out of the Word of the Lord. The more you search the Scriptures, and the nearer you live to God, the more you will enjoy of that great goodness which the Lord has laid up in store for them that fear Him. Though 'eye hath not seen, nor ear heard, the things which God hath prepared for them that love him,' yet 'he hath revealed them unto us by his Spirit,' and thereby He puts gladness into our hearts more than increasing corn and wine could bring.

Furthermore, *faith gives cheering interpretations.* Faith is a prophet who can charmingly interpret a fearsome dream. Faith sees a gain in every loss, a joy in every grief. Read aright, and you will see that a child of God in trouble is on the way to greater blessing. Faith views affliction hopefully. Sorrow may come to us, as it did to David, as a chastisement for sin. Faith reads, 'Whom the Lord loveth he chasteneth, and scourgeth every son whom he receiveth.' Better to be chastened with God's children here than to be condemned with the world hereafter. Faith also sees that affliction may be sent by way of discovery, to make the man know himself, his God, and the promises better. Faith perceives that affliction may be most precious as a test, acting, as doth the fire, when it shows what is pure gold and what is base metal. Faith joys in a test so valuable. Faith spies out the truth, that affliction is sent to develop and mature the Christian life. 'Ah, well!' saith Faith, 'then, thank God for it. No trial for the present seemeth to be joyous, but grievous; nevertheless, afterwards it worketh out the peaceable fruit of righteousness in those that are exercised thereby.' Faith sees sweet love in every bitter cup. Faith knows that whenever she gets a black envelope from the heavenly post-office, there is treasure in it. When the Lord's black horses call at our door, they bring us double loads of blessing.

Up to this moment I, God's servant, beg to bear my unreserved testimony to the fact that it is good for me to have been afflicted. In spiritual life and knowledge and power, I have grown but little except when under the hand of trouble. I set my door open, and am half-inclined to say to pain and sickness and sadness, 'Turn in hither; for I know that you will leave a blessing behind. Come, crosses, if you will; for you always turn to crowns.' Thus faith glories in tribulations also, and in the lion of adversity finds the honey of joy. I have said that trial comes to us as chastisement, as we see in the case of David; as a discoverer of grace, as we see in Abraham; or as a test, as we see in Job; or as a preventive, as in the case of Paul, who wrote, 'Lest I should be exalted above measure through the abundance of the revelations, there was given to me a thorn in the flesh, the messenger of Satan to buffet me.' In every tribulation God is moved by love to His people, and by nothing else. If He cuts the vine with a sharp knife, it is because He would have fruit of it. If He whips His child till he cries like David, 'All the day long have I been plagued, and chastened every morning,' it is for his profit, that he may learn obedience by the things which he suffers. All things work together for the believer's good, and so faith interprets sorrow itself into joy.

Moreover, *faith believes great promises.* This opens other wells of joy. I cannot stop to quote them to you this morning: the Book of the Lord is full of them. What more can the Lord say than He hath said? The promises of God are full, and as varied as they are full, and as sure as they are varied, and as rich as they are sure. 'Exceeding great and precious promises.' When I wrote *The Cheque Book of the Bank of Faith* I was at no loss to find a promise for every day in the year; the difficulty was which to leave out. The promises are like the bells on the garments of our Great High Priest, for ever ringing out holy melodies. When a man gets a promise fairly into the hand of faith, and goes to God with it, he must rejoice. The children of the promise are all of them worthy to be called Isaac, that is 'Laughter'; for God hath made him to laugh who lives according to promise. To live on the promises of man would be starvation; but to live on the promises of God is to feed on fat things full of marrow.

Above all, *faith has an eye to the eternal reward.* She rejoices in her prospects. She takes into her hand the birds which to others are in the bush. To be with Christ in the glory land is the joy of hope, the hope which maketh not ashamed. Our hope is no dream: as sure as we are here today, we who are trusting in Christ will be in heaven before long; for He prays that we may be with Him where He is, and may behold His glory. Let us not wish to postpone the happy day. Shall our bridal day be kept back? Nay, let the Bridegroom speedily come, and take us to Himself. What a joy to know that this head shall wear a crown of glory, and these hands shall wave the palm branch of victory! I speak not of myself alone, my brethren, but of you also, and of all them that love His appearing. There is a crown of life laid up for you, which the righteous Judge will give you. Wherefore, have patience a little while. Bear still your cross. Put up with the difficulties of the way, for the end is almost within sight.

The way may be rough, but it cannot be long:
So we'll smooth it with hope, and cheer it with song.

May the Lord give us the ears of faith wherewith to hear the bells of heaven ringing out from afar over the waters of time!

Faith has always reason for joy, since God is always the same, His promises are the same, and His power and will to fulfil are the same. In an unchanging God we find unchanging reasons for joy. If we draw water from the well of God, we may draw one day as well as another, and never find the water abated; but if we make our joy to depend in part upon creatures and circumstances, we may find our joy leak out through the cracks in the cistern. Last Sunday morning I cried out to you, 'Both feet on the rock! Both feet on the rock!' and the words led one poor heart to try the power of undivided faith in God. This is the road to joy, and there is no other. Drink waters from thine own fountain, and do not gad abroad after others. Is not the Lord enough for thee? Is it not sufficient to say, 'All my fresh springs are in thee'? Neither life, nor death, nor poverty, nor sickness, nor bereavement, nor slander, nor death itself, shall quench thy joy if it be founded in God alone.

We will look, for a minute or two, into a third matter, which is **the failures reported concerning this joy**. I think I hear somebody say, 'It is all very well for you to tell us that believers are joyful, and have logical reasons for gladness; but some of them are about as dull as can be, and create dullness in others.' I am obliged to speak very carefully here, for I am afraid that certain Christians give cause for this objection.

Let me say to some of you who love to raise objections, *What do you know about this joy?* Are you unbelievers? Well, then, you are out of court: you are not competent to judge. The griefs of believers you do not know, and with their joy you cannot intermeddle. You have no spiritual taste or discernment, and what judgment can you form? A genuine believer may be as happy as the angels, and yet you may not know his joy, because you are not in the secret. You have not a spiritual mind, and the carnal mind cannot discern spiritual things. I would have you speak with bated breath when you talk on this matter. When a blind man goes to the Royal Academy, his criticisms on the pictures are not worth much; but they are quite equal in value to yours when you speak of spiritual things. You cannot know what joy in the Lord may mean; for, alas! you a stranger to such heavenly things.

Alas! *some professors of religion are mere pretenders*, these have no joy of the Lord. To carry out their pretence, these persons even imagine that it is necessary to pull a long face and to talk very solemnly, not to say dismally. Their idea of religion is, that black is the colour of heaven. But, dear friends, we cannot prevent hypocrites arising; it is only a proof that true religion is worth having. You took a bad half sovereign the other night, did you? Did you say, 'All half sovereigns are worthless, I will never take another'? Not so: you became more careful, but you were quite sure that there were good half sovereigns in currency; for else people would not make counterfeit ones. It would not pay anybody to be a hypocrite unless there were enough genuine Christians to make the hypocrites pass current. Therefore, do not say too much about hypocritical weepers, lest you slander true men.

Next, remember that *some persons are constitutionally sad*. They cried as soon as they were born; they cried when they cut their teeth; and they have cried ever since. Their spirits are very low down, and when the grace of God gets into their hearts it lifts them a great deal to bring them up to a decent level of joy. Think of what they would have been without it. Many would have died in despair, if it had not been for faith. The grace of God has kept them up, or they would have lost their reason. I am sorry there should be persons who have bad livers, feeble digestions, or irritated brains; but there are such. Pity them, even if you blame them. They must not so pity themselves as to make an excuse for their unbelief; but we must remember that often the spirit truly is willing, but the flesh is weak.

When you have met with Christians who are not happy, did it never strike you that their *depression might only be for a time* under very severe trial? You may go to the south of France, where the days are so sunny, and you may happen to be there for a couple of days only, and it may rain all the time. It would be unfair on that account to say that it is a gloomy place. So it may be that the Christian is under extreme pressure for the time, and when that is moderated he will be very joyful. I do not excuse his loss of joy; but, still, there is a November of fogs in the year of most men. Judge no man by the day, but watch his spirit on a larger scale, and see whether he does not usually delight himself in God.

Moreover, I would like to say a very pointed thing to some people who charge the saints with undue sadness. *May you not be guilty of making them so?* There is an unkind, morose, wicked, drinking husband, and he says, 'My wife's religion makes her miserable.' No. It is not her religion, but her husband. You are enough to make twenty people unhappy: you know you are; and therefore do not blame the poor woman, if, when she sees you, the tear is in her eye. Alas! when she thinks of your going down to hell, and knows that she will be parted from you for ever, the more she loves you the more sad she is to think of you. 'Oh,' says some wild boy here, 'my mother is wretched!' I do not wonder; I should be wretched too, if you were my son. If any of you are living ungodly lives, it makes your parents' hearts ache to see you going headlong to perdition. Is it not abominable that a man should make another miserable, and then blame him for being so? If you were but saved, how your mother's face would brighten up! If your father saw his boy turn to the Lord, he would be as happy as the birds in spring. Speak tenderly on this matter lest you accuse yourself.

If you say that some Christians are unhappy, *must you not also admit that many of them are very happy?* I was once waited upon by an enthusiast who had a new religion to publish. Numbers of people have a crack which lets in new light, and this man was going to convert me to his new ideas. After I had heard him, I said, 'I have heard your story, will you hear mine?' When I talked to him of my lot and portion in the love of a covenant God, and the safety of the believer in Christ, he said, 'Now, sir, if you believe all this, you ought to be the happiest man in the world.' I admitted that his inference was true; but then I said to him, what rather surprised him, 'So I am; and I am going to be more so all the rest of my life.' If a man is chosen of God from before the foundation of the world, is redeemed by the precious blood of Christ, is quickened by the Holy Ghost, and renewed in the spirit of his mind, is one with Christ, and on his way to heaven; if he is not happy, he ought to be. Surely, we ought to rejoice abundantly, dear friends, for ours is a happy lot. 'Happy are the people whose God is the Lord.'

If God's people are not happy at times, *it is not their faith which makes them unhappy* – ask them. It is not what you believe that makes you unhappy, it is your want of faith, is it not? If a man begins to doubt, he begins to sorrow: so far as his faith goes, he has joy. Oh, for more faith! Faith does create joy. We can answer all objections by the fact that 'we that have believed do enter into rest'.

I close by mentioning **the arguments for abounding in joy.** You cannot argue a man into gladness, but you may possibly stir him up to see that which will make him happy.

First, you see in my text *a permit* to be glad: 'Let all those that put their trust in thee rejoice.' You have here a ticket to the banquets of joy. You may be as happy as ever you like. You have divine permission to shout for joy. Yonder is the inner sanctuary of happiness. You cry, 'May I come in?' Yes, if by faith you can grasp the text, 'Let all those that put their trust in thee rejoice.' 'But may I be happy?' asks one. 'May I be glad? May I? Is there joy for me?' Do you trust in the Lord? Then you have your passport; travel in the land of light.

But the text is not only a permit, it is *a precept*. When it says, 'Let them shout for joy,' it means that they are commanded to do so. Blessed is that religion wherein it is a duty to be happy. Come, ye mournful ones, be glad. Ye discontented grumblers, come out of that dog-hole! Enter the palace of the King! Quit your dunghills; ascend your thrones. The precept commands it: 'Rejoice in the Lord alway: and again I say, Rejoice.'

We have here more than a permit and a precept, it is *a prayer*. David prays it, the Lord Jesus prays it by David. Let them rejoice, let them be joyful in thee! Will He not grant the prayer which He has inspired by causing us to rejoice through lifting upon us the light of His countenance? Pray for joy yourself, saying with David, 'Restore unto me the joy of thy salvation.'

The text might be read as *a promise*: 'All those that put their trust in thee shall rejoice.' God promises joy and gladness to believers. Light is sown for them: the Lord will turn their night into day.

Listen to the following line of argument, which shall be very brief. You only act reasonably when you rejoice. If you are chosen of God, and redeemed by blood, and have been made an heir of heaven, you ought to rejoice. We pray you, act not contrary to nature and reason. Do not fly in the face of great and precious truths. From what you profess, you are bound to be joyful.

You will best baffle your adversaries by being happy. David talks about them in both these psalms; but he does not fret, he simply goes on rejoicing in God. 'They say; they say': let them say! 'Rest in the Lord, and wait patiently for him.' But the attack is cruel. No doubt it is, but the Lord knows all about it. Do not cease to rest in Him. If your heart is full of God's love, you can easily bear all that the enemy may cast upon you. Abound in joy, for then you will behave best to those who are round about you. When a man is unhappy, he usually makes other people so; and a person that is miserable is generally unkind, and frequently unjust. It is often dyspepsia that makes a man find fault with his servants and wife and children. If a man is at peace with himself, he is peaceful with others. Get right within, and you will be right without. One of the best specifics for good temper is communion with God, and consequent joy of heart.

You yourself also, if you are happy, will be strong: 'The joy of the Lord is your strength.' If you lose your joy in your religion, you will be a poor worker: you cannot bear strong testimony, you cannot bear stern trial, you cannot lead a powerful life. In proportion as you maintain your joy, you will be strong *in* the Lord, and *for* the Lord.

Do you not know that if you are full of joy you will be turning the charming side of religion where men can see it? I should not like to wear my coat with the seamy side out: some religionists always do that. It was said of one great professor, that he looked as if his religion did not agree with him. Godliness is not a rack or a thumbscrew. Behave not to religion as if you felt that you must take it, like so much physic, but you had rather not. If it tastes like nauseous physic to you, I should fear you have got the wrong sort, and are poisoning yourself. Believe not that true godliness is akin to sourness. Cheerfulness is next to godliness. 'When thou fastest, anoint thine head, and wash thy face, that thou appear not unto men to fast.' Weed out levity, but cultivate joy. Thus will you win other hearts to follow Jesus.

Remember, that if you are always joyful, you are rehearsing the music of the skies. We are going there very soon, let us not be ignorant of the music of its choirs. I should not like to crowd into my seat, and hear the choirmaster say, 'Do you know your part?' and then have to answer, 'Oh, no, I have never sung while I was on earth; for I had no joy in the Lord.' I think I shall answer to the choirmaster, and say, 'Yes; I have long since sung, "Worthy is the Lamb."'

> I would begin the music here
> and so my soul shall rise:
> Oh, for some heavenly notes, to bear
> my passions to the skies!

With joy we rehearse the song of songs. We pay glad homage now before Jehovah's throne. We sing unto the Lord our gladsome harmonies, and we will do so as long as we have any being. Pass me that score, O chief musician of the skies, for I can take it up and sing my part in bass, or tenor, or treble, or alto, or soprano, as my voice may be. The key is joy in God. Whatever the part assigned us, the music is all for Jesus.

May some of you that have never joyed in Jesus Christ learn how to praise Him today by being washed in His precious blood! You that have praised Him long, may you learn your score yet more fully, and sing in better tune henceforth, and for evermore! Amen.

5

The Joy of Holy Households[1]

'The voice of rejoicing and salvation is in the
tabernacles of the righteous: the right hand of the
Lord doeth valiantly. The right hand of the Lord is
exalted: the right hand of the Lord doeth valiantly.'
(Ps. 118:15-16)

A believer in Christ is not long without finding joy. He is in the land which floweth with milk and honey, and he will get a sip of sweetness very soon. Like Nicodemus, he comes to Jesus in the dark, but the sun is rising. When he casts himself at the foot of the cross, his dawning has begun, and before long he will walk in the light: being justified by faith, he will have peace with God. And not only so, for he

---

1. Preached at the Metropolitan Tabernacle, Newington, in connection with the dedication of the Jubilee House, which commemorated the completion of the beloved Pastor's fiftieth year, June 10th, 1884.

also learns to joy in God, through our Lord Jesus Christ, by whom also he has received the atonement. This joy is in him and abounds, so that he belongs to a happy people. It is true that all believers are not equally happy, but they have each one of them a right to be exceeding glad. Some float upon a flood-tide of joy, while others drift upon the ebb; but they are all in the same stream, and it is bearing them on to the ocean of perfect felicity. All who trust in Christ as they ought to do will find a measure of this joy springing up within them, keeping company with the new life which the Holy Spirit has created. Ours is peace which passeth all understanding, and joy unspeakable.

This joy is contagious; it spreads like a sweet perfume. The happy man makes others happy. The man who is full of the blessedness of God overflows for others. Music is not alone for him who maketh it, but for all who have ears. The happy man's influence is first felt at home; he goes home to his own family a converted man, and they soon perceive the change. He tells them of what the Lord has done; but even if he did not do so, they would soon discover by his gentleness, his love, his truth, his holiness, that something remarkable had happened to him. His actions, his words, his temper, his spirit, are singularly altered, and those around him can see it. He is glad, and before long they are glad, too. When the man is better, everybody who belongs to him is the better for his improvement. When the man's own heart rejoices, he distributes joy, even as Christ's disciples; when they received bread and fish from the hands of their Lord, they divided them among the multitude, 'and they did all eat, and were filled.'

I trust that many of you, dear friends, who are my associates in the church of God, feel this to be true in your own cases, as I am sure I must confess it to be true in mine. To the glory of God's grace I must give the testimony. Our own God of blessing has blessed our families. Certain believers, however, spread joy through a large number of families; not only those to which they belong according to the flesh, but among all the families of Zion they scatter comfort. David, for instance, when he went forth, and smote the enemies of his nation, caused great rejoicing in all the tabernacles of Israel; all the chosen people shared in what the champion of the Lord had done. When any man is blessed of God, so that he can teach the Word, and preach it with power, he sheds joy over all the families with which he comes in contact. Aspire, dear brethren, to shine widely, as a candle set upon a candlestick giveth light to all that are in the house. First, see to it that you are truly saved yourselves; then cry to the Lord for your own kith and kin, and labour for them till they are all brought to the Redeemer's feet; and then let your light shine throughout the neighbourhoods wherein you dwell.

It is a poor lamp which cannot be seen outside its own glass. Shine down that street from which so few ever go up to the house of God; shine in that factory where the mass of the workers sit in darkness; shine in that bank, where few of the clerks are walking in the light of God. Pray that you may be, not merely night-lights to comfort one sick person, but like those new gas-lamps, which are placed at the crossroads, and make a grand illumination all round. It may be that the Lord has placed you in a trying position on purpose that you may be of more service than you could have been under more comfortable circumstances. We ought to be happy to be where we can make others happy. It should be our will to do the Lord's will by being useful to our fellowmen. We must not value our position according to the ease it brings to us, or the respectability with which it surrounds us, but by the opportunities which it affords for overcoming evil, and promoting good.

I think that many Christian people would be wise to hesitate before they remove from the place where they now are, even though it would be very agreeable to them to live in a more reputable locality. I say that they might hesitate to remove, because, if they were gone, the very light of the place would be quenched, and the hope of many poor sinners would be removed. Salt can never do so much good in a box as it can effect upon meat, which else would corrupt. A pilot on shore may be very clever, but he cannot be useful unless he goes to sea. A river is a blessing in England, but it is beyond measure prized in Egypt or the Sudan; the Scriptures speak of 'rivers of water in a dry place'. Let us pray that we may be such men and women that we may bless our own households, and then may be so located in providence that, to the utmost of our capacity, we may be channels of blessing to an ever-widening circle, of which we are the centres. Oh, for a share in the benediction which fell on Abraham, 'In blessing I will bless thee;' and again, 'I will bless thee, and make thy name great; and thou shalt be a blessing;' and yet again, 'And in thy seed shall all the nations of the earth be blessed.'

We will now press more closely to the text, and we notice in it, first, that *there is joy in the families of the righteous*. The text says so, and experience and observation confirm it; and secondly, *this joy should be expressed*: 'The *voice* of rejoicing and salvation is in the tabernacles of the righteous.' Then, thirdly, *this joy concerns what the Lord hath done:* 'The right hand of the Lord doeth valiantly. The right hand of the Lord is exalted: the right hand of the Lord doeth valiantly.'

First, there is **joy in the families of the righteous**. Thank God, that is divinely true. Once, paradise was man's home; and now, to the good man, his home is paradise. I may say that, to some extent, *this is in proportion to the salvation that is found in the family.* If one or two persons be converted out of a numerous family, it is a thing for which to praise God, that He takes 'one of a city, and two of a family,' to bring them to Zion; yet the joy will be rather a soft melody than an exulting harmony. If the wife shall be converted as well as the husband, what a comfort it is to them both! Now will two parts of the music be taken up, and the hymn will be more sweetly sung. If two horses in a chariot pull together, how well it rolls along; but if one backs and the other pulls, there will be discomfort, if not mischief. I have seen two oxen in a yoke, and I have marked how the true yokefellows seek to accommodate each other, so as to lie down together, rise together, and move in step together; where it is not so, the pain and inconvenience make it hard ploughing.

If the husband and the wife are both converted, a larger joy is yet within their reach, for they will begin to pray for their children. Those who are born to them will be their anxious care till they are also born unto God. They will have great delight, when one of their dear ones says, 'I have given my heart to Christ,' and is able to express his faith in Jesus, and to give a reason for the hope that is in him. It will further fill their cup of pleasure when another comes, saying, 'I would be numbered with Christ's flock.'

Many among us can say, 'All my children are children of God; they go with me from my table to the Lord's table; I have a church in my house, and all my household are in the church.' Here is a picture, a pattern, a paragon, a paradise. We may say what a minister of Christ once said of his spiritual children, 'I have no greater joy than to hear that my children walk in truth.' It is better, dear father, dear mother, that your boys and girls should be heirs of God than that you should be able to make them heirs of a vast estate; it is better that they should be good than great; better that they should be gracious than famous. If they are married to Christ, you need not fret about finding them husbands; and if they serve the Lord, you need not worry about their businesses. While you live, they will be your comfort; and when you die, you will leave them in better hands than your own. Their future is well secured, since it is written, 'Instead of thy fathers shall be thy children, whom thou mayest make princes in all the earth.' I think it is generally true that the joy in a family is very much in proportion to the grace which is in its members. Circumstances and peculiar trials may cause exceptions to the rule, but in the main it will hold good. Seek, then, the salvation of the whole of your household.

Here it would be a sad omission if I did not say that it is a greater joy when the saved circle includes, not only the parents and the children, but the servants also. A gracious, faithful servant is a great comfort; and to be surrounded by those who fear the Lord is one of the choicest blessings of this mortal life. We ought not to be content, so long as a single domestic in our house is unconverted. The nursemaid, the girl who comes in for part of the day, the boot-cleaner, and all who are employed occasionally for extra work, should be thought of by the mistress and the fellow-servants. We should pray that all who set their foot over our threshold may have a name and a place in the house of our God. Why should it not be? May we not often chide ourselves that we have been forgetful of those who minister to our comfort? Oh, that all who serve us may serve God! May all who wait at our table eat bread in the kingdom of our Father, and may all who dwell under our roof have a place in the many mansions above!

Now we advance a step, and remark that the joy which is here alluded to is mainly spiritual. To fear God, tends to make a man happy in every way, mentally, physically, socially, as well as spiritually. It is light to the eyes, music to the ears, and honey to the mouth. It is universally a sweetener. The ordinary work of life runs easily when the wheels are oiled with grace. It should be an ambition that our house should be a temple, our meals sacraments, our garments vestments, ourselves priests unto God, and our whole life a sacrifice to His praise. There are households where the Lord Jesus is the Master both of master and servants, and the Holy Spirit is the presiding spirit in the whole economy of the house. Difficulties that disturb others never occur there, for love prevents them. All are gracious; all are anxious to be good, and to do good, and to get good. Consequently, jars and strifes are unknown; little differences are never allowed to grow into disputes. Envyings and bickerings and clamour and evil speaking are put away; though these spring up even among those who are of the same kin, yet gracious hearts will not tolerate their existence. Each pays due consideration to each; proper places are kept according to New Testament rule, and the result is that the angel is in the house, and the devil sees the mark upon the door, and dares not enter.

> Blessed is the man that feareth,
> And delighteth in the Lord,
> Wealth, the wealth which truly cheereth
> God shall give him for reward;
> And his children,
> Shall be blest around his board.

Yes, the chief joy in the tabernacles of the righteous is a spiritual one; a joy of the father, because he is saved in the Lord with an everlasting salvation; a joy of the mother, because she, too, has had her heart opened, like Lydia, to hear and to receive the Word; a joy of the dear children, as they offer their little prayers, and as they talk of Jesus, whom their soul loves. I do not know that I ever have a greater joy than when, sometimes, I have to receive a whole family into the church. Five came to see me at one time from one house – quite a company of boys and girls. It is delightful to see our beloved offspring early in life giving their hearts to the Lord. Happy mothers, happy fathers, happy brothers, happy sisters, where the Lord works so graciously! May you long continue to praise and bless His name for this singular blessing, if you are partakers in it! I know none of my father's family, or of my own, who are unsaved; and therefore I can lead you in the song.

This kind of joy, while it is spiritual, is *not dependent upon external circumstances;* it hangs not on wealth or honour. The joy of the Lord will be found in the palace of a prince, if the grace of God be there; but far oftener it flourishes in humble cottages and lowly rooms, where

Christian men are dwelling who toil hard for a livelihood, and often feel the pinch of poverty. They said of old that philosophers could be merry without music, and I am sure that it is truer still of Christians that they can be happy in the Lord when temporal circumstances are against them. Our bells need no silken ropes to set them ringing, neither must they be hung in lofty towers. If our joy depended upon heaping together gold and silver, or upon the health and strength of all the members of our family, or upon our rank and pedigree, we might go to our beds weeping, and awake in the morning blinded with tears; but as our joy springs from another well, and the precious drops of it distil from a purer fount, whose streams flow both in summer and winter, we can bless God for a constancy of satisfaction.

Steady is that flame of joy which burns in the tabernacles of the righteous, for it is fed with holy oil. God grant that we may never dim its lustre by family sins towards God, or by negligence in our duties to one another; but may the sacred lamp of holy joy continually shed its radiance upon us from generation to generation! May it be said of our habitation, 'Jehovah Shammah' – 'the Lord is there.'

I heard of a wealthy man who had a large number of houses in various places. He owned a fine estate in the country, surrounding a magnificent mansion; he kept up an establishment at the West End, a retreat by the seaside, and a shooting-box in the Highlands, and he would often travel on the Continent. He wandered from house to house, and was never known to stop more than a few weeks in any one residence. He told a friend that he was trying to find peace of mind in some one or other of his houses. What a vain quest! He might as soon have found the philosopher's stone, or the universal solvent. I have known many persons who had only one room, and that but poorly furnished, yet they found peace of mind there, because they carried it about with them.

Happy is the man who wears the emerald of peace upon his bosom, even though it be not set in gold. Blessed are they whose peace is like a river, having a source far away in the hills, and a stream clear as crystal, continuous, ever-deepening, ever-widening, moving silently onward toward the ocean of boundless felicity. Yes, it is not where we are, but what we are; and it is not what we have, but where we have it, whether we have it in ourselves or in our God, that proves whether we are truly blessed. Peace is the best possession for an individual, the richest estate for a family, and the fairest legacy for descendants. Where the salvation of our Lord Jesus comes, peace and joy are sure attendants: therefore is it said in our text that 'the voice of rejoicing and salvation is in the tabernacles of the righteous'. Made righteous in character, we may more than ever feel the temporary nature of our earthly sojourn, and so may dwell rather in tabernacles than in mansions; but we are honoured by the companionship of these two heavenly guests – salvation and joy, and therefore we envy no Caesar on the Palatine Mount, no monarch in his palace of marble.

Christian joy, whether in the individual or the family, *can be abundantly justified.* Believers can always give a reason for the joy which is in them. As Christian households, why should we not be glad in the Lord? If God is pleased with us, we may well be pleased with Him. If the Lord rejoices over us, ought we not to rejoice in that fact? God Himself calls us a happy people; let us not live as if we would falsify His Word. See, my brothers and sisters, whatever your temporal troubles may be, all things are working together for your good; may you not, therefore, rejoice evermore? Though every drug that is put into the mixture may be bitter, yet the whole potion is salutary; though each event may seem to be against you, yet the whole course of providence is for you in a divinely-wise and gracious manner. Nothing occurs in your family history, whether of birth or death, of coming or departure, of loss or of gain, of joy or of sorrow, of sickness or of health, but what shall produce in the end the highest good. Judge not each wheel, but watch the outcome of the whole machinery. To me, it is a happy thought that not a grain of dust in the March winds, nor a drop of rain in the April shower, is left to chance, but the hand of the Lord directeth all; and therefore am I confident that neither in the little nor in the great shall anything really harm the man who dwells under the protection of the Most High.

Beside this, we rejoice in forgiven sin; this is the first blessing of which David sings in the hundred and third Psalm, and it is the preparation for all the rest. If sin be pardoned, all bitterness is past, for this is the real wormwood and gall of life. Now that Goliath of Gath is smitten in the forehead, the rest of the Philistines are of small account. When sin is gone, the black cloud which threatened an eternal tempest, is removed, and the sun scatters the rest of the clouds as it disperses the morning mist. Even death has lost its dread when sin is gone; it is a bee without a sting, and we look to find honey near it. If it comes into the house, and takes away our dear ones, they are with Christ, which is far better; and when it bears us away, our death will be gain, for 'so shall we ever be with the Lord'. As the whole of life receives another colour when sin is pardoned, so does death itself look otherwise to the believer in Jesus; that solemn business is so altered that we may even –

Long for evening to undress,
That we may rest with God.

What is there upon earth to trouble you who fear God? 'Why,' say you, 'we could tell you of a thousand trials.' Yes, but when you had done, I would tell you that there was no ground for being troubled about any one of them; for it is written, 'No weapon that is formed against thee shall prosper.' 'No good thing will he withhold from them that walk uprightly.' And again, 'All things are yours, whether Paul, or Apollos, or Cephas, or the world, or life, or death, or things present, or to come; all are yours, and ye are Christ's, and Christ is God's.' 'They are the seed of the blessed of the Lord, and their offspring with them.' Wherefore, let us take care that we be not as the Egyptians when they shivered in the darkness which might be felt, but rather as the people were in the days of Solomon, when they ate and drank and made merry, and peace was without end.

I would ask any of you young people who are newly-married, and just starting in life, how can you expect happiness unless you seek it in God? You have given your hearts to one another; oh, that you had given your hearts to Christ as well, for then you would be joined in One from whom you can never be separated! If you are one in Christ, you will have surer grounds of union than natural affection can afford. There will be a brief separation of the body when one of you is taken home; but you will meet again, and dwell for ever in the same heaven. Unions in the Lord are unions which have the blessing of the Lord. See to it that you begin as you mean to go on; namely, with that blessing which maketh rich, and brings no sorrow with it. If your home is to be happy, if the children that God may give you are to be your comfort and your delight, first let your own souls be right with God. If the Lord be the God of the parents, He will be the God of their seed. The God of Abraham will be the God of Isaac, and He will be the God of Jacob, and He will be the God of Joseph, for He keeps His faithfulness from generation to generation of them that love Him. He does not cast off His people, nor their children either. If you are an Ishmael, what will your children be? If you are far from God, how can you hope that your posterity will be near unto Him?

To return to my first point, the people of God are a happy people, and their families are happy families. If I have any Christian person here who complains, 'I am not happy at home,' I would like to inquire, 'Is that your own fault, dear friend?' Nay, do not be angry, I am bound to ask the question, for I often find that those who complain of unhappiness in their own homes are the main cause of that unhappiness. Most creatures see according to their nature, and men often get into their bosoms what they measure out to others. When I meet a man who cries, 'There is no love in the church,' you may turn that expression into plain English, and read it thus, 'There is no love in me.' When a person says, 'Everybody at my home is wrong except myself,' you feel sure that he has kept his eyes open to the faults of others, but has never really seen himself. If you wear coloured spectacles, all things around you will be coloured.

'Alas!' cries another, 'I am not happy, though I long to be so.' Do you know, dear friend, the secret of obtaining happiness? The answer is very simple; do not attempt to make yourself happy, but endeavour to make others so. Be cheerful, and cheer those about you. I bless God that I never fell into the delusion that there is virtue in a rueful countenance. Some may think it well to be 'miserable sinners', but surely it is better to be happy saints. Carry sunshine about with you in all ill-weather. Do not think that in godliness *drive* will be equal to *draw*. A frown may benefit a few, a smile will influence more. A famous French statesman had such a dreadful countenance that a boy once asked him whether his face did not hurt him. Surely some very 'proper' people might be asked the same question, for they habitually wear such gloom about them that one would think that all was night within. Let it not be so with us, but let the light of love be round about our path causing flowerets of cheerfulness to spring up on every side. There are enough weeping willows by all our streams; I would they were fuller of water-lilies. More grace would enable us to glory more in the Lord, and rejoice with more constant joy.

So much for our first witness: there is joy in the families of the righteous.

Secondly, **this joy should be expressed**: 'The voice of rejoicing and salvation is in the tabernacles of the righteous.'

We should put a tongue in our joys, and let them speak. The voice should be heard daily, from morn till eve, and till the silence of sleep steals over all; but it should never fail to sound forth *in the daily gatherings for family prayer*.

It should be a happy occasion when we meet to read the Word of God, and to pray together. It is well if we can also sing at such times. Matthew Henry says, concerning family prayer: 'They that pray do well; they that pray and read the Scriptures do better; they that pray, and read the Scriptures, and sing a hymn, do best of all.' Herein he was wise and gracious as usual; I wish that his words received more attention. If you cannot compass the last of the three good things, mix the praise with your prayer by making it fuller of joy and thankfulness than is usual. Never let the domestic devotion degenerate into a dull formality, but throw a hearty living delight into it, so that there shall be joy in drawing near unto the Lord, and not a weariness in it. Where there is no family prayer, we cannot expect the children to grow up in the fear of the Lord, neither can the household look for happiness.

Perhaps some of you have not begun family prayer, for you have only lately been converted. Commence it at once, if possible; let not this day end without an attempt at it. But I hear a man say, 'I never did pray aloud.' Then begin at once, my brother. 'But I am afraid.' Are you afraid of your wife? That assuredly is a great pity; I am very sorry for your manhood, for she is the last woman of whom you should be afraid. 'Oh, but I should break down!' That might be no great calamity; a break-down prayer is often the best form of supplication. May not this objection arise from pride? You do not like to pray before your family unless you can do it well, and so receive their approbation. Shake off this spirit, and think only of God, to whom you are to speak. Language will follow desire, and before long you will have to be more afraid of your fluency than of your brevity. Only break the ice; pray the Lord Jesus to cast out the dumb spirit, and He will set you free from its power.

If the husband will not lead the devotion, let the wife do it; but let no day pass without family prayer; a house without it, is without a roof; a day without it, is without a blessing. Do you say to me, 'Alas! dear sir, my husband is not converted'? Then, my dear sister, endeavour to have prayer with the children, and pray yourself. I remember, when my father was absent preaching the gospel, my mother always filled his place at the family altar; and in my own family, if I have been absent, and my dear wife has been ill, my sons, while yet boys, would not hesitate to read the Scriptures and pray. We could not have a house without prayer; that would be heathenish or atheistic.

There will be frequent occasions for holy joy in all Christian families, and these ought always to be used right heartily. Holy joy breeds no ill, however much we have of it. You can easily eat too much honey, but you can never enjoy too much delight in God. Birthdays and anniversaries of all sorts, with family meetings of various kinds, should find us setting life to music right heartily. Moreover, it would be well *if our houses more generally resounded with song.* It drives dull care away, it wards off evil thoughts, it tends to a general exultation, for the members of a household to be accustomed individually and collectively to sing. Of course, there must be common sense in this as in all other things, but as worldlings are able to sing songs, we might with no more difficulty sing psalms. I have known some very happy people who were always humming psalms, and hymns, and spiritual songs. I knew a servant who would sing when washing, and she said it made the work grow lighter. It is a capital thing to sing when you are at work.

Keep on 'tooting' a little, if you cannot sing; that is a word I got from an old Primitive Methodist. I used to meet him in the morning; he was toot-toot-toot-tooting as he went along the road. When he was at work in the field, it was just the same. I asked him what made him always sing. He replied, 'Well, I don't call it singing, it is only tooting; but it is singing to me, it is singing in my heart; I sing in this fashion because I feel so happy in the Lord. God has saved me, and put me in the road to heaven, why should I not sing?' What a noise we sometimes hear from the wicked when they are serving their god! They make night hideous with their songs, and shoutings, and blasphemies; then why should not we make a joyful noise unto the Lord our God? I recommend you to try, in your own houses, literally to Praise the Lord with your voices in holy song.

If you really cannot sing at all, yet the voice of rejoicing and salvation may be in your tabernacles _by a constant cheerfulness,_ bearing up under rain and poverty, losses and crosses. Do not be cast down, beloved child of God; or, if you are, chide yourself about it, and say, 'Why art thou cast down, O my soul? and why art thou disquieted in me? hope thou in God: for I shall yet praise him for the help of his countenance.' Joy is the normal condition of a Christian; when he is what he should be, his heart rejoices in the Lord. Does not the apostolic command run thus, 'Rejoice in the Lord alway'? If you ever get outside that word 'always', then you may leave off rejoicing; but that you cannot do, therefore obey Paul's injunction, 'Rejoice in the Lord alway: and again I say, Rejoice.' Heap the joys one on the top of another; joy and rejoice, and then rejoice yet again.

Why should the children of a King
Go mourning all their days?

Why should not the children of the King of kings go rejoicing all their days, and express their joy so that others shall know of it, too? Ah, dear friends, if we were to go into some people's houses where God is not known, we should hear a very different sound from the voice of rejoicing and salvation! There is the drunkard's horrible voice that grates upon the ear of her whom he promised to love and cherish, but whose life he makes unutterably miserable, while even the little children run upstairs to get out of the drinking father's way. It is an awful thing when a house is like that; and there is many a house of that kind; and in other places, where there is no drunkenness, there is many a man, without the fear of God, who comes in and blusters and bullies as if everybody had to be his slave. There is a woman, perhaps, who is a sloven and a slattern, making the home wretched through her gossip and idleness, and driving all idea of happiness far away. These things ought not to be, and they must not be. God grant that your house may not be like that; but may whoever comes into your house be compelled to know that God is there, and to know it mainly by the fact that you are a happy, joyful, cheerful, thankful Christian, speaking well of God's name, and not ashamed in any company to avow that you are a soldier of the cross, a follower of the Lamb! God give you more and more of this spirit in all your households! The whole church shall be blessed when every family is thus made happy in the Lord and in His great salvation.

I close by briefly noticing that this joy of holy house-holds **is a joy concerning what the Lord hath done**. You see, dear friends, that I have a text which is too large to be handled in one sermon, so we must have the remain-der another day. But I must ask you to notice the song the holy households sing; it is this: 'The right hand of the Lord doeth valiantly. The right hand of the Lord is exalted: the right hand of the Lord doeth valiantly.' It is a three-fold strain; we and our children have learned to bless the Triune God. 'Glory be to the Father, and to the Son, and to the Holy Ghost; as it was in the beginning, is now, and ever shall be, world without end! Amen.'

How we should joy in God, in our families, when we *think of all that He has done* in conquering sin and Satan, death and hell! Christ hath led captivity captive; therefore, let us sing unto the Lord, for He hath triumphed gloriously. In that great victory of His upon the cross, truly the right hand of the Lord was exalted, the right hand of Jehovah-Jesus did valiantly on our behalf, and for that we ought for ever to be glad and to praise His name.

Then let us think of *what the Lord has done for each one of us individually.* We were captives under the dominion of sin and Satan, but He brought us out with a strong hand, and with a stretched-out arm, even as He delivered Israel from the Egyptians. Then our sins pursued us, and we were ready to despair; but the Lord again wrought our deliverance, and plucked us from the hands of our mighty foes, and set us gloriously at liberty. Truly, 'the right hand of the Lord doeth valiantly.'

Since then, the Lord has *helped us in providence, and delivered us from fierce temptations,* and made us to stand steadfastly when the adversary has thrust sore at us that we might fall. 'The right hand of the Lord is exalted: the right hand of the Lord doeth valiantly.' As I look back upon my own life, I never know where to begin in praising God; and, when I begin, I am sure I do not know where to leave off. 'O my soul, thou hast trodden down strength!' In thy case also, dear friend, the right hand of the Lord has been exalted in giving thee strength in the midst of weakness, and helping thee despite thy many falls and failures; cannot you each one in your separate sphere see something that the right hand of the Lord is doing for you? Do you not, therefore, think that your families ought to ring with joyous songs of thanksgiving?

When the work of the Lord is prospering, when you go home from a church meeting after many have confessed their faith in Christ, when you see the pool of baptism stirred by many who have come to be symbolically buried with Christ, when you see the church breaking out on the right hand and on the left, new mission stations and Sunday schools being opened, and more workers busy for the Master, should not your hearts dance for joy as you sing, 'The right hand of the Lord doeth valiantly. The right hand of the Lord is exalted: the right hand of the Lord doeth valiantly'?

And when you see great sinners converted, when the drunkard leaves his cups, when the swearer washes out his filthy mouth, and sings the praises of God, when a hardened, irreligious, sceptical man bows like a child at Jesus' feet, should not our families as well as ourselves be made acquainted with it, and should it not be a subject for joy at the family altar? I am sure that it should be; and when you hear the missionaries reporting their success, when the heathen turn to the Lord, and the nations begin to receive the light of Christ, should we not then have a high day of jubilee, and say, 'This is the day which the Lord hath made; we will rejoice and be glad in it'? I want our families to participate more and more in the joy of the great family of God, till our little families melt into the one great family in heaven and earth, till our separate tribes become part of the one great Israel of God, till we and all our kith and kin are one body in Christ, and praise that Lord who is our glorious Head.

Ah, dear friends, but we must each one begin by exercising personal faith in the Lord Jesus Christ! Some who are here do not yet know the Lord. You cannot make other people happy while you are yourself without the true secret of happiness; yet you wish to be a fountain of blessedness to others, do you not? You do not desire to do them hurt, do you? Yet you good moral people, who do not yield your hearts to God, do a great deal of mischief if your conduct leads other people to say, 'It is quite enough to be moral and upright; there is no need for us to go to Christ, to confess our sin, and to receive from Him a new heart and a right spirit.' You make them talk thus by setting them such an evil example. As for you who go in and out of the house of prayer by the year together, and scarcely ask a blessing upon your meals, much less call your children to your knee to tell them about Christ, remember that you will have to meet those children at the Day of Judgment. What will they say to you parents if you neglect their souls? You work very hard, perhaps, to earn their daily bread, and to put clothes on their backs, and you love them very much; but that is a poor love which loves only the body, and does not love the real child, the soul that is within. If, in the middle of the night, someone woke you up, and said, 'Your Johnny is not at home,' there would be a stir in the house pretty quickly; there would be no sleep for you if little Johnny was out in the cold.

I wish that I could wake up some of you parents who are saved, but who have children who are not converted. Do pray that they may be saved before they leave your roof. The other day, I saw a woman who came to join the church, and her great sorrow was that her children were all ungodly, and she could not speak to them now as once she might have done when they were in her own house. She never sought their salvation then, and that time was over, for they were men and women grown up, and they paid but little respect to a mother's word. I always like to hear what two children told me only a fortnight ago. One said, 'I found peace at my mother's knee,' and the next one said, 'I found peace with God at my mother's knee.' A mother's knee is a charming place for a child to find the Saviour; let your knees be thus consecrated till your children shall there draw nigh unto God. Will you not take them individually, and pray with them, and speak to them about their souls? If you do, I think that I can venture to promise you that you shall succeed in almost every case.

Whenever I hear of the children of good people turning out badly, if ever I have had an opportunity of searching into the cause, there has generally been a good reason for it. I heard of a minister's sons who were all bad fellows; but when I began to look into the life of the family, I wondered how that minister dared enter the pulpit at all, for his own character was not such as would be likely to lead his children to the Saviour. It may not be so in every case; but I believe that, where there is family prayer, and a happy home, and a holy example, and much earnest supplication with and for the children, Solomon's declaration is still true, 'Train up a child in the way he should go: and when he is old, he will not depart from it.'

O dear friends, may my text come true to all of you! The Lord grant it, for Jesus' sake! Amen.

6

Joyful Anticipation of the Second Advent

'And when these things begin to come to pass, then look up, and lift up your heads, for your redemption draweth nigh. And he spake to them a parable; Behold the fig tree and all the trees, when they now shoot forth, ye see and know of your own selves that summer is now nigh at hand. So likewise ye, when ye see these things come to pass, know ye that the kingdom of God is nigh it hand.'
(Luke 21:28-31)

I have already said that I conceive our Lord Jesus Christ to have regarded the destruction of Jerusalem as 'the beginning of the end'. Although some eighteen hundred years have rolled away since that terrible event, we with Him may make but small account of the interval, and regard it all as one dispensation of passing away. That beautiful city was the very crown of the entire earth, because God had dwelt there. It may be compared to the diamond in a ring, the jewel whose setting was the whole world; and when that jewel was destroyed, and God did as it were grind it to powder, it was a warning that the ring itself would, by-and-by, be crushed and consumed; for 'the heavens shall pass away with a great noise, and the elements shall melt with fervent heat, the earth also and the works that are therein shall be burned up.' The destruction of Jerusalem was, so to speak, the uprolling of the curtain on the great drama of the world's doom; it will not fall again until all the things that we now see shall have passed away, and only the things that cannot be shaken – the things of God and of eternity, which we cannot see – shall remain.

Moreover, I think that, from this chapter, if we are to understand it all – and it is confessedly very difficult to comprehend – we must regard the siege of Jerusalem and the destruction of the temple as being a kind of rehearsal of what is yet to be. God's long-suffering was displayed with Israel for centuries. The rebellious tribes had ample space for repentance. They had even been carried away into captivity; and, by the Lord's gracious lovingkindness, they had struggled back again; yet, only changing the form of their apostasy, they continued to wander away from God. They were bent on backsliding from Jehovah even when their idols were all destroyed, and the seed of Abraham had come to hate every sort of symbol and image. Yet, then, they began to set up other kinds of idols in the traditions of the fathers, and the inventions of the scribes. Thus they lost the spirit of divine teaching in the mere letter of it, and became only formalists when they ceased to be idolaters; for, mind you, the truth, if it be dead, has no more virtue in it than falsehood has. When the Spirit of God is gone out of that which in itself is right, it becomes often a cover wherein a thousand evils conceal themselves. So, at last, God's longsuffering had come to an end, and, according to current tradition, there was a sound as of the moving of wings in the holy place at Jerusalem; and it is reported that one priest, who stood to officiate at the altar, heard the solemn sentence, 'Let us go hence,' for God was about to leave His temple. That temple had already rent its veil from the top to the bottom for very shame at what had been done to the Lord Christ; and now the fabric itself must be consumed with fire, even in spite of the order of the Roman emperor. With all his power, he could not save it from ruin, and so completely was the city destroyed that Zion was ploughed as a field, and the very site of the temple was for many a day a question in dispute.

Ah, my friends, this was a picture – a faint picture – of what shall be the case when the Lord Jesus Christ shall come again! Then, all external religion, if it be but external, shall perish in the fire, and only the spiritual and the true shall live. 'For, behold, the day cometh, that shall burn as an oven; and all the proud, yea, and all that do wickedly, shall be stubble and the day that cometh shall burn them up,' as it was with the temple fabric. In the day that is coming, that only shall endure upon which fire can have no power, that only shall stand which is God's own eternal truth. So, then, I regard that destruction of Jerusalem and its temple as the beginning of the end, and also as the rehearsal of what is yet to be.

The times before the destruction of Jerusalem were terrible to the last degree. If you have read Josephus, you cannot but feel your heart bleed for the poor Jews. They were utterly infatuated, they were so carried away with heroic madness that they fought against the Romans with a desperate valour, after the city had been surrounded. Never upon this earth were there braver or more fanatical spirits than were those who were cooped up within those city walls. When they were weary with fighting the Romans, they turned their swords and their daggers against one another, being divided into sects and parties who hated each other with the utmost fury. Jerusalem was a cauldron, a boiling pot, seething full of all manner of evil, and mischief, and misery.

The land was devoured before the Roman armies. Everybody seemed to be either driven from the country, or else to be left dead around the city walls. They crucified the Jews in such numbers that they left off doing it because they could find no more wood upon which to nail them. Those who were taken captive were sold for slaves till a penny was refused as their price; they literally sold them for a pair of shoes. The precious sons of God, as the prophet said, comparable to fine gold, were esteemed as earthen pitchers, cracked and broken, and only worthy to be thrown upon the dunghill.

But all the time – the most awful time, perhaps, that any nation ever endured – the disciples of the Lord Jesus Christ were altogether unharmed. It is recorded that they fled to the little city of Pella, were quiet according to their Master's command, and not a hair of their head perished. Indeed, it was to them a time of redemption, for the persecution which the Jews had carried on against them had been exceedingly cruel, and now there was a pause. Their own miseries were so great that they had no care nor thought for the poor Christians; they at least were secure, they looked up, and lifted up their heads, for their Master's prophecy was verified, and the full force of the curse fell upon those who had cried to Pilate, 'His blood be on us and on our children.'

Now, dear friends, it will be just so at the last. I am not about to enter into any prophecies of what is yet to be, but here are the Master's own words: 'There shall be signs in the sun, and in the moon, and in the stars; and upon the earth distress of nations, with perplexity; the sea and the waves roaring; men's hearts failing them for fear, and for looking after those things which are coming on the earth: for the powers of heaven shall be shaken. And then shall they see the Son of man coming in a cloud with power and great glory. And when these things begin to come to pass, then look up, and lift up your heads; for your redemption draweth nigh.'

That is my subject, dear friends; and we will consider, first, *the terrible time in which this precept is to be carried out*: 'Look up, and lift up your heads;' secondly, *the remarkable precept itself*: 'Look up, and lift up your heads;' and thirdly, *the encouraging parable* which is given in order to induce us to look up, and lift up our heads: 'Behold the fig tree, and all the trees; when they now shoot forth, ye see and know of your own selves that summer is now nigh at hand. So likewise ye, when ye see these things come to pass, know ye that the kingdom of God is nigh at hand.'

First, then, here is **a terrible time**, in which we are told to look up, and lift up our heads. It is evidently to be a time of *fearful national trouble*; and if such times should ever come in our days – if there should ever arrive times that are worthy to be compared with the destruction of Jerusalem – here is the Master's word to us, 'When ye shall hear of wars and commotions, be not terrified: for these things must first come to pass; but the end is not by and by.' Should great wars occur, as they certainly will, there is nothing in them to terrify the Christian. Should they even come to your own doors, it is not for believers in Christ ever to be the victims of a scare. Whatever may happen, what is there for them to fear? The Saviour gives them this precept for a time when it will be impossible for them to carry it out unless it be by faith in Him: 'Look up, and lift up your heads.' Whatever chastisements shall befall the nations, you shall be secure in following to the full the principles of peace that your Master has enjoined upon you.

Further, this precept is given, not only in times of fearful national trouble, but also in times of *awful physical signs and wonders in the world*: 'There shall be signs in the sun, and in the moon, and in the stars.' It may be a season of preternatural darkness; or the solar system may be disturbed, so that the stars of heaven, which have been fixed for centuries, shall fall like unripe fruit from the trees, or as the withered leaves of autumn are scattered by the stormy blast. You know that, when there is some phenomenon such as they have never seen, and such as their fathers have never seen, how frightened people are! But suppose there should be visible in the heavens manifestations such as have never been seen before, yet even at such times the children of God are to look up, and lift up their heads, and if they should not merely be in the heavens, but if the earth also should shake and tremble – if that which is supposed to be most stable should become most fickle – yet even then we are to look up, and lift up our heads. And if the sea and the waves thereof should roar in a manner altogether unusual, so that landsmen should hear the noise afar off, or if, being out at sea ourselves, the waves should run mountains high, and the vessel should threaten to sink to the bottom, yet still this is the precept for the worst of times that are supposable: 'When these things begin to come to pass, then look up, and lift up your heads.' Even in such a trying time as that, take up the language of the forty-sixth Psalm, and say, 'God is our refuge and strength, a very present help in trouble. Therefore will not we fear, though the earth be removed, and though the mountains be carried into the midst of the sea; though the waters thereof roar and be troubled, though the mountains shake with the swelling thereof.'

'Nature cannot rise to that height,' says one. No, I know it cannot; but grace can. 'I cannot rise to it,' says one. Perhaps you cannot, but there is One who can raise you up to it, and it is He Himself who bids you so to rise. 'Then,' says Jesus, 'when these things begin to come to pass, *then* look up, and lift up your heads.'

This terrible time which our Lord describes is, in addition, a time of *universal alarm*: 'Upon the earth distress of nations, with perplexity; men's hearts failing them for fear, and for looking after those things which are coming on the earth: for the powers of heaven shall be shaken.' You know that fear is contagious; when one person trembles, many begin to feel the same sort of tremor; and when all the people, wherever we shall go, at home or abroad, shall be in distress – when everywhere the hearts of men shall seem to die within them, or turn as it were to stone, so that they cannot act or move, like those who guarded the tomb of Christ, who, when they saw Him rise, were as dead men – if it should ever come to that, and there should be a general panic, then you who have Christ for your Master, God for your Father, eternity for your heritage, and heaven for your home, even then you may 'look up, and lift up your heads.'

You ask, perhaps, 'How shall we do that?' You cannot do it without your Lord. With God, all things are possible. In Christ, you can do all things; without Him, you can do nothing. If you live away from your Lord and Master, in those days of terror that are yet to come, your hearts will quail for fear, and you will be like other men. If you run with them, you shall fear with them. If your strength is where their strength is, you shall be as weak as they; but if you have learned to look up, why, even in those stormy times you shall keep to the habit of looking up; and if you have learned to lift your heads above the world, you shall keep to the habit of lifting up your heads. If your portion is in heaven, it shall not be shaken when the earth rocks and reels to its very foundations; if your treasure is in heaven, then your treasure shall not be lost.

If God be with you, you can stand between the very jaws of death, or in the centre of hell itself, and feel no fear. With Christ by your side, you may be as calm amid the wreck of matter, and the crash of worlds, as your Lord Himself is in His glory. He can work even this in you if you do but cast yourself on Him, and live wholly to Him.

Once more, the time when we are to be thus calm and quiet, and to look up, and lift up our heads, is to be at *the coming judgment*. My dear brothers and sisters, whatever I might say to you about the calamities that are yet to come upon the earth, whatever description I might give of wars, and earthquakes, and storms – if I were to make each word as black as night, and each sentence as sharp as a killing sword – yet could I not fully describe the final scene when the Lord Himself shall come in all the pomp and splendour of the last dread assize. No human tongue can tell, as no human heart can imagine, the terrors of that tremendous day, especially the sight of the once-crucified King when He appears seated upon His great white throne, and when the summons shall ring out,

> Come to judgment!
> Come to judgment, come away!

when the grave shall not conceal the unnumbered dead, nor even the depths of the ocean suffice for a hiding-place from Him that sitteth upon the throne, for all shall be gathered before Him, every eye shall see Him, and they also that pierced Him. You will be there, my friend, you will be there as certainly as you are here. O you who are without Christ, all the fear and dread you have ever had in this life will be as nothing compared with the alarm and terror of that day! Your fears when you have been laid low with fever, and have been near to death's door, will be but as child's play compared with what you will feel at that tremendous day which is soon to come. Yet Christ says to His people, concerning even that time of terror, 'look up, and lift up your heads.' There is nothing for you who have put your trust in Him, ever to fear. It is your Judge who is coming, but He comes to acquit you, and to exhibit you to the assembled universe clad in His own righteousness which you already wear. He who is coming is your Lord, your Friend, your Bridegroom; He who has sworn to deliver you is coming to call your body from the grave, and to raise you up to dwell together with Himself for ever. That day of Christ's appearing shall be to you a morning of the ringing out of harps, and a time of joyous shouts and blissful songs.

There shall be weeping, there shall be weeping,
At the judgment-seat of Christ;

but not for you who are in Him; it shall be your joy day, your wedding day, the brightest day in all your history. 'When these things begin to come to pass, then look up, and lift up your heads.'

I must leave this first point, concerning the terrible time when this precept is to be carried out, by just reminding you that, when the Lord Jesus Christ shall come, the heavens shall tell us: 'There shall be signs in the sun, and in the moon, and in the stars.' The earth shall tell us, for upon the earth there shall be 'distress of nations, with perplexity.' The sea shall tell us, for the sea and the waves thereof shall roar. Men shall tell us, for men's hearts shall fail them for fear, and for looking after those things which are coming on the earth. And then, as all these voices shall proclaim His coming, our own eyes shall tell us, for they shall see 'the Son of man coming in a cloud with power and great glory.' 'Then shall the righteous shine forth as the sun in the kingdom of their Father'; and in anticipation of that glorious day, each believer can say with the patriarch Job, 'I know that my Redeemer liveth, and that he shall stand at the latter day upon the earth: and though after my skin worms destroy this body, yet in my flesh shall I see God: whom I shall see for myself, and mine eyes shall behold, and not another.'

Now I come to **the remarkable precept** itself: 'Then look up, and lift up your heads.' My dear brethren, there are some Christian people who seem to think that it is almost wicked to look up, and lift up their heads. When they come before God, their cry is, 'Lord, have mercy upon us, miserable sinners.' Well, but surely a true child of God gets above that condition. He is a sinner, it is true; and as far as he is a sinner, he is unhappy; but still, he has been regenerated by the Holy Ghost, he has been washed in the blood of the Lamb, he has been adopted into the family of God, so surely there is some nobler note for him to reach than that doleful dirge. If, amid plague and pestilence, or amid earthquakes and storms and wars, we are to look up, and lift up our heads, that ought to be our daily attitude.

Why does your face, ye humble souls,
Those mournful colours wear?
What doubts are these that waste your faith,
And nourish your despair?

Listen to your Lord's gracious command: 'Look up, and lift up your heads.' What does this precept mean? First, it implies an _absence of fear_. 'Perfect love casteth out fear: because fear hath torment.' He that feareth is not made perfect in love. What cause has a Christian for fear? What is there that can harm the man whom God loves? Will He trample on His child, or allow anyone else to hurt him? Nay; for 'all things work together for good to them that love God, to them who are the called according to his purpose.' The sun and moon and stars, the earth and the seas, wars and pestilences, all work together for good to God's dear children. Let us therefore cast out all fear.

This precept, surely, also means _the removal of all grief_. While the Christian is here, there will always be more than enough to make him grieve as a man; but there will also always be grace in Christ to wipe every tear away. We are born to grief; but then we are also born again, so we must not give way to weeping more than is right, we must not be overburdened with sorrow, lest we become like a man drunken. It is as evil to be drunken out of the bitter cup of affliction as out of the sweet cup of sinful pleasure. Let us put away our sorrow, and grief, and misery, and say, with the prophet Habakkuk, 'Although the fig tree shall not blossom, neither shall fruit be in the vines; the labour of the olive shall fail, and the fields shall yield no meat; the flock shall be cut off from the fold, and there shall be no herd in the stalls: yet I will rejoice in the Lord, I will joy in the God of my salvation.'

'Look up, and lift up your heads.' This precept of our Lord seems to me to be very wonderful, because it does not merely mean that there is to be in believers no fear and no grief, but that, *even in the worst times, we are to show the signs of joy*. This expression implies to me signs and tokens of an outward kind: 'Look up, and lift up your heads.' Our Lord seems to say to us, 'Now fly your flags, and ring your bells; let your hearts be exceeding glad, so joyous that those who look at you cannot help seeing your happiness.' 'Look up, and lift up your heads.' Let there be no looking down because the earth is quaking and shaking, but let there be a looking up because you are going to rise from it; no looking down because the graves are opening; why should you look down? You will quit the grave, never more to die. 'Lift up your heads.' The time for you to hang your heads, like bulrushes, is over already, and will certainly be over when the Lord is coming, and your redemption draweth nigh. Wherefore, 'look up, and lift up your heads.'

It will be a wonderful sight when Jesus comes again. It must have been a wonderful sight when Jerusalem was destroyed, but the true Christian knew all that was going to happen; and all that did happen, terrible as it was, was only a confirmation of his faith, and a fulfilment of his Lord's prophecies. So shall it be when, at the last great day, we walk among the sons of men calmly and serenely. They will marvel at us; they will say to us, 'How is it that you are so joyous? We are all alarmed, our hearts are failing us for fear;' and we shall take up our wedding hymn, our marriage song, 'The Lord is come! The Lord is come! Hallelujah!' The burning earth shall be the flaming torch to light up the wedding procession; the quivering of the heavens shall be, as it were, but as the dancing of the feet of angels in those glorious festivities, and the booming and crashing of the elements shall, somehow, only help to swell the outburst of praise unto God the just and terrible, who is to us our exceeding joy.

I cannot speak as I would upon this glorious theme, but I think I catch some of our Master's meaning when He said, 'Then look up, and lift up your heads.' Did He not mean that then, and always, Christians are to be filled with *an inward peace* and with a *holy expectancy* mixed with it? Whatever happens, all is well with the righteous. I know not what is to be, nor do I wish to know; but I know that all is well, and that all shall be well for ever and ever. 'Look up, and lift up your heads,' beloved, for it is better on before. There is something brighter and more joyful coming than we have ever yet known. All our earthly bliss is but as the vestibule of our eternal delights. The Lord's kingdom is yet small and feeble, apparently; but it is to be world-wide, and He Himself is to be manifested in His glory. Therefore, let us look up, and lift up our heads. Look up for Him who is coming, look up for Him who has already come. Lift up your eyes unto the hills, whence cometh your help. 'Look up, and lift up your heads.' It seems to me as if the text itself is quite enough to make you march to the strains of martial music straight away to victory. Come, let us be a band of men who fully trust our Lord, and who henceforth say farewell to doubt and trembling, 'Look up, and lift up your heads.'

Our text finishes with a **parable to encourage us to obey the precept**: 'Behold the fig tree, and all the trees; when they now shoot forth, ye see and know of your own selves that summer is now nigh at hand.'

First, notice the *signs* mentioned in this parable. Summer is the time of the bursting of buds, the unfolding of flowers, the forming and ripening of the fruit. There may come many a shower in the springtime, but that will not hinder the arrival of summer; rather will it help summer to come. It may be cold and chill beneath the black cloud that hovers over us for a while; but that will not hinder summer. 'April showers bring forth May flowers.' All these things are the tokens of the summer's coming. So, brethren, when you are in trouble, expect that you are going to have a blessing. When you are passing through a great trial, look out, for there is another sign that summer is coming. Do not fear to look up, and lift up your heads, for —

> The clouds ye so much dread
> are big with mercy,
> and shall break
> in blessings on your head.

'Look up, and lift up your heads.' I wish we could get into the habit of believing that every time of want, every time of pain, every time of depression, is but the commencement of a season of blessing. 'Though now for a season, if need be, ye are in heaviness through manifold temptations,' remember that the Lord's object in this experience is 'that the trial of your faith, being much more precious than of gold that perisheth, though it be tried with fire, might be found unto praise and honour and glory at the appearing of Jesus Christ.' Therefore, as you look at the black buds on the tree of your life, say to yourself, 'I wonder what bright flower is coming out there!'

Look at the dark bulbs, without any beauty at all in them, which we put into the ground, yet the flowers which come out of them are charming and fragrant. So, when God plants some black bulbs in the garden of your soul, do not cry out because of their ugliness, but look for the flowers that shall in due time appear, and expect something beautiful from God's sowing. Ay, and if again the heavens should be darkened, and the earth should shake, and the sea should roar, and kingdoms should be dissolved, and pestilence should slay its myriads, yet still 'look up, and lift up your heads.' Your Master bids you do so. He, the Crucified, who made a coronet of beauty out of the crown of thorns, He who is bedecked today with jewels which are the scars of His own suffering, He whose very glory it is that He once died, He it is who would have you see, in as the trials of the present hour, tokens of the benediction that is yet to come. Wherefore, 'look up, and lift up your heads.'

Further, the signs mentioned in this parable tell of *certainty*. When the trees are in bloom, hastening to display their leaves, there may come a frost, there may come many cold days, there will certainly come rough winds and clouds, but the summer will come all right in due time. Every day will bring it nearer. All the devils in hell cannot keep the spring from going on to summer; it is not possible, the forces of nature are by God so ordained that the trees must come to their perfection at the crowning of the year; and, in like manner, the signs that God gives to His people, though they may not always seem promising, are very sure. Have you trusted in Christ? Then, to you He has given peace and joy. Are you still trusting Him, and will you continue to hang alone upon Him, and to trust wholly in Him? Then, your righteousness shall break forth as brightness, and your salvation as a lamp that burneth. The Lord will light your candle. The night may be very long, but the morning must come when the Sun of righteousness shall rise upon you with healing in His wings, and you shall 'go forth, and grow up as the calves of the stall.'

As for the coming of our Divine Master, and the triumph of everything that is right and true, as to the fulfilment of his covenant, and the perfecting of all his everlasting purposes, as for the salvation of his elect and redeemed ones, heaven and earth may pass away, but his Word shall not pass away till every jot and tittle of it shall be fulfilled. God is with you, God is in you, and who can stand against Him? Trust you in the Lord, even in the mighty God of Jacob, and you shall never be ashamed nor confounded, world without end. Go your way, and say, 'All is well, for it is in my Father's hands; therefore will I look up, and lift up my head.'

And, as for you who are not His people, begin to look out for a place to hide yourselves, for Christ is coming.

O ye earth-worms, begin to look for the holes into which you will wish to creep to hide yourselves! I wish that you would so look out for a hiding-place that you would find one in that Man who presents Himself as the best hiding-place for every sinner who will trust Him. God bring you as to find refuge in Christ! Amen.

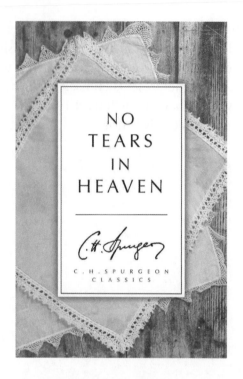

No Tears in Heaven

C. H. Spurgeon

No Tears in Heaven speaks of the great joy of the Christian faith
– Heaven. This book brings together, in a new way, a number of
Charles Haddon Spurgeon's exhilarating teachings on Heaven.
The writings of Spurgeon, in his typically beautiful and pen-
etrating style, will deepen our anticipation of Heaven and chal-
lenge us to a closer walk with God.

ISBN: 978-1-78191-404-5

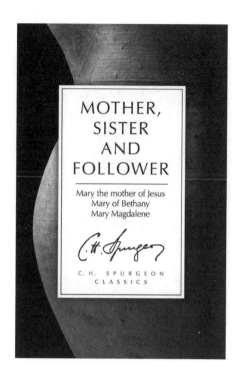

MOTHER, SISTER AND FOLLOWER

Mary the Mother of Jesus, Mary of Bethany,
Mary Magdalene

C. H. Spurgeon

Reflecting on the life and influence of the Marys of the Bible, an often neglected theme, Spurgeon illustrates their role and significance but never loses sight of the Saviour they loved. This book brings together some of C.H Spurgeon's illuminating reflections on Mary the mother of Jesus, Mary of Bethany, and Mary Magdalene.

ISBN: 978-1-78191-405-2

Spurgeon's Sorrows

Realistic hope for those who suffer from depression

Zack Eswine

Christians should have the answers, shouldn't they? Depression affects many people both personally and through the ones we love. Here Zack Eswine draws from C.H. Spurgeon, 'the Prince of Preachers' experience to encourage us. What Spurgeon found in his darkness can serve as a light in our own darkness. Zack Eswine brings you here, not a self-help guide, rather 'a handwritten note of one who wishes you well.'

ISBN: 978-1-78191-538-7

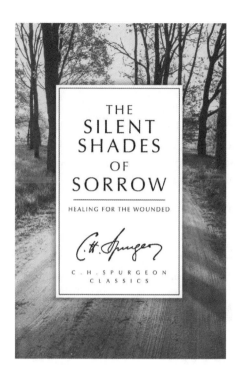

The Silent Shades of Sorrow

Healing for the Wounded

C. H. Spurgeon

Pastor Charles Spurgeon was a friend to those who physically and mentally suffered. He and his own dear wife, Susannah, suffered truly through years of physical and mental pains. In this light, Charles preached transparently about sorrows and their many kinds, including depression in all of its forms. He was no trite preacher. He spoke as one who had been there.

This collection of works from C. H. Spurgeon offers a healing taste of his powerful ministry on our sorrows.

ISBN: 978-1-78191-585-1

Christian Focus Publications

Our mission statement –

STAYING FAITHFUL
In dependence upon God we seek to impact the world through literature faithful to His infallible Word, the Bible. Our aim is to ensure that the Lord Jesus Christ is presented as the only hope to obtain forgiveness of sin, live a useful life and look forward to heaven with Him.

Our books are published in four imprints:

CHRISTIAN
FOCUS

Popular works including biographies, commentaries, basic doctrine and Christian living.

CHRISTIAN
HERITAGE

Books representing some of the best material from the rich heritage of the church.

MENTOR

Books written at a level suitable for Bible College and seminary students, pastors, and other serious readers. The imprint includes commentaries, doctrinal studies, examination of current issues and church history.

CF4•K

Children's books for quality Bible teaching and for all age groups: Sunday school curriculum, puzzle and activity books; personal and family devotional titles, biographies and inspirational stories – because you are never too young to know Jesus!

Christian Focus Publications Ltd,
Geanies House, Fearn, Ross-shire,
IV20 1TW, Scotland, United Kingdom.
www.christianfocus.com